'It Rains I_____ n memoir in the form of a _____ ceased husband. The prose is stunning and lush, rich with detail. As a reader, I could smell the flowers, the coffee, the cigarettes, the sea, and the death. The characters are richly drawn and undeniably real. One cannot help but be moved by the immense sacrifice this woman is willing to make for this man, her family, and the meaning of life, death and love. Summers also shows a biting grasp of the language. E-mails passed between the characters provide the reader with a wildly intimate look at a couple struggling with every duality imaginable: love and loss, joy and madness, friendship and intimacy and, ultimately, life and death. It will leave you questioning the meaning we attach to all of it. It Rains In February reads as a wrenching yet uplifting, brutal and gentle, hopeless and life-affirming story. If you're like me, you'll want to start it again as soon as you finish the first read.'

– Dr. John Duffy, clinical psychologist and author

'Leila Summers has written a memoir that takes you completely into her world. Saved emails and intimately personal diaries cried out to be crafted into a book, and Summers has not let them down. Her vivid images draw the reader into the room with the abandon of a movie-goer watching a fine film. She portrays her husband's agony and behavior with the clarity of an observer yet the compassion of a loving wife. Summer's indomitable spirit provides testament to the power of the heart to rise above tragedy and embrace hope.'

– Dr. Deborah Barry, Happiness Coach and author

It Rains In February

A Wife's Memoir of Love and Loss

Leila Summers

'Farewell at Vetch's Pier' is courtesy of Kobus Moolman. First published in *Durban in a Word: Contrasts and Colors in eThekwini*. Penguin Books, 2008. Edited by Dianne Stewart.

ISBN-13: 978-1-463-76359-6
ISBN-10: 1-463-76359-X

Cover Design by Roger Jardine
Photograph by Dave Southwood

http://www.leilasummers.com

Printed in the United States of America

For Jane and Rose

Preface

Exactly three years have passed since you chose to leave this world. This morning, as I edged through the thin veil between dreams and daylight, Jane and Rose were at my bedside, both talking at once. Slowly, consciousness set in, and their garbled words made sense.

"Mom, the goldfish is dead."

Dead. Two wide-eyed little girls peered intently down at me. With a drowsy smile that softened their worried faces, I said, "Well, he was very old. It was his time."

Poking the bloated orange scales, I confirmed their diagnosis: definitely dead. Carefully, I scooped him out of the water and made my way to the toilet with the girls following closely behind. A few seconds of silence prevailed, and then, we watched him circle the bowl and get sucked away.

"Find your way to the sea, little fellow, and find peace," I croaked. Then, we went about our day as if it were any other day.

Jane and Rose don't know the significance of dates and times. They have little idea about the details of that dreadful year that led up to your suicide or the grief that took me afterwards. I wrote this book for them, so that they will someday know all that took place, however painful the details may be to comprehend. Our stories are a part of who we are.

Through the cathartic process of writing and reliving my story, I walked through my own grief and hurt, into a voyage towards self-discovery and healing.

I have done my best to detail events as accurately as I could from memory, with the help of journal entries, letters, and e-mail messages. Mostly, the two years of which I write are imprinted on my heart, ingrained like hieroglyphics chiseled in stone – things I will never forget and do not want to.

Names and a few minor identifying details have been changed, so as not to hurt anyone with my words. E-mail messages and letters are authentic. I've written under the nom de plume Leila Summers for reasons that will become clear as you read. I am Robyn and this is my story.

PART I

1

You slump to the ground on the veranda, hold your head in your hands, and begin to weep. My skin feels hot. I start trembling even though it's a sweltering summer evening in the South African coastal city of Durban. The veranda wraps around two sides of our old Victorian wood-and-iron house in the suburbs. It is trimmed with white wooden lace and a railing that we added as soon as Jane could crawl.

"I'm so in love," you choke through sobs.

Your pause exists outside of time, suspended in the humid air.

"I can't lie to you any longer, Robyn. I just... I love Amanda so much."

Syllables fall at my feet like tiny pieces of shattered glass. Two white French doors lead from the veranda into the large entrance room where I stand speechless, trying to put the bits together. The room is spacious with a high molded ceiling and wooden paneled walls, painted in white and mint green stripes. Crammed into the bookshelves are Marquis de Sade, Anaïs Nin, Bukowski, Hemingway, Dostoyevsky, Sartre, and your other favorite authors. A large painting by your ex-girlfriend hangs conspicuously on the wall. Everything stops.

It's Wednesday, middle of the week, Wednesday the 1st of February 2006. Early this morning, our daughters Jane and Rose, aged five and three, flew to Johannesburg with Amanda's husband Barry. Our families have become close during the past two years; our eldest children are best friends. Barry had offered to escort the girls on the one-hour flight with him, so that they could visit my parents for a holiday. I was thrilled at the thought of having you all to myself, even after being married for seven years. You arrived home from work in a foul mood. Hurling your cell phone across the entrance room, you ranted about a phone call you had received on your way home. Amanda had called to warn you that rumors were going around town regarding the two of you. She had suggested that you visit her to discuss the situation. With Barry away on a business trip and their two sons in bed, you would be alone with her. Immediately suspicious, I suggested coming along. That was when you sank to the ground. I watched you in slow motion. Then, I heard the words that would change my life forever.

In other houses, people are eating spaghetti and bathing children. My world is motionless.

You mutter something about going to Amanda's house to end it. End what? I think, but two other words slip out of my mouth, "How long?"

"Since the beginning. I'm so sorry, Robyn."

A rough calculation tells me that it is over two years since the day you met Amanda at music rehearsals. Our youngest daughter, Rose would have been only a year old. All of a sudden, I see the scene from outside of myself. I become an onlooker, watching somebody else's movie. This cannot be happening to me. My hands don't feel like my own as I reach for my keys. Lifting your head slowly you ask, "Where are you going?"

"I don't know," I manage in a voice I do not recognize. My reality collapses with each step I take. Further away from familiarity, from all I know and trust.

My car somehow finds its way to my dear friend Lisa's house.

She pours me a generous glass of wine. While relaying my short story, I realize that I don't actually know any details. Nothing makes sense.

Lisa is one of my oldest friends in Durban. Her long blond curls are wild and bouncy like her gypsy Gemini spirit. We met years ago while waitressing and remained close through boyfriends and fiancés, marriage and children. After several glasses of wine, Lisa offers me a lift home. She reassures me that I can collect my car in the morning, when the whole thing will probably be sorted out. I experience a moment of optimism, telling her that this could all be a misunderstanding. Surely you aren't really in love with Amanda. Perhaps this is just a midlife crisis. You will most likely visit her tonight and discuss your feelings logically. Then you will come to realize that I am the one you truly love. That it's been me all along. Lisa agrees, in an effort to console me.

Your motorbike isn't at home yet, so Lisa suggests a drive past Amanda's house, just to take a look. I think her idea is pointless, but oblige since driving is better than going inside the empty house alone.

Parking a block away, we sneak up the road on foot. We can't see or hear anything over the high wall surrounding Amanda and Barry's house on the corner. We find your bike, stashed away in an abandoned park down the side road. I feel as if I am in a B-grade detective movie. Lisa, bless her, is by this time smoking a fat joint that she thinks is an essential addition to our stakeout. She hands it to me as she heads to the front of the house for a closer inspection. As she disappears around the corner, you come running out of the garage door on my side, to check on your motorbike. You must have heard us. In fright, I manage to duck into a neighbor's doorway, unspotted, and shift back to blend into the shadows as you run across the road. By this time, the joint in my hand, which is still burning, is puffing out billows of smoke from my dark doorway. If you don't see the smoke, you will surely smell it. I barely breathe as you walk back towards the garage and slip inside. A slightly hysterical titter escapes my lips. I can't cry now. I still have hope. This nightmare could soon be over. I want to go home.

I wait in the doorway for what seems like hours for Lisa. She doesn't come. Eventually, I run back down the road to her car where I find her puffing and panting. Apparently, she had such a scare when you came out that she started running down the street, and finding no hideout to escape into, she kept running for three blocks until she finally reached her car from the other direction. With feeble giggles, we retreat and drive home, having accomplished nothing.

Lisa waits with me in her car outside our house until we hear your motorbike. She squeezes my hand encouragingly and leaves. I follow you down the long stairway and onto the veranda, where we sit down uncomfortably. Unsure of what to say, I relay my detective story, and we chuckle a bit. The momentary laughter gives way to silence.

It is dark except for the yellow garden light that casts an odd shadow across your resolute jaw. I clutch my fingers to control the shaking. For a while, the only sound is the shrill screech of bats from the trees above. I want to find out details, but at the same time, I don't. Over the years, you had made some radical statements late at night when you were drunk about things you renounced or apologized for the following day. I wonder if this could be one of those times. But this night is not like the others. Everything has changed; the old rules don't apply.

You break the silence by admitting that after crying buckets of tears together with Amanda, you couldn't do it. Neither one of you could bear to end whatever it is that you have. I ask another question that I'm not sure I want an answer to. "So, what do we do now?"

"I'll move out."

More words. They travel slowly towards me. This is the point of no return. They suck out my last hope, and I am left feeling withered and broken. I watch as you leave the veranda to go inside, to climb into the bed we once shared in love.

It has started to rain, and I wonder how I will ever sleep again. I miss the girls terribly, but am thankful they aren't here now. There is a stranger in my bed. He wants to leave me tomorrow. A thought niggles at me. In the brief moment I saw you outside Amanda's house, I thought I noticed that you weren't wearing any shoes. Am I wrong? What does this mean? Does one end a whatever-it-is in socks?

2

My eyes fly open, and at once, I become fully conscious, aware that things aren't normal. Glancing across the bed, I examine your wiry blond hair buried into the pillow and the familiar worry creases etched on your face. Your chest moves rhythmically up and down with your breath. I linger, desperately wanting to stay in a moment where other possibilities exist, other outcomes. To pause here, or rewind back to any day besides this one, a day before you met her. A time when you were still in love with me.

But the morning plays out as I dread. Sipping coffee in shell-shocked silence, I avoid looking into your eyes for fear of what I won't see. Without a word, you kiss my forehead and leave for work. The habitual gesture makes me wince. The house appears quieter than it has ever been. Emptier.

Without thought or purpose, I sit down in front of my computer. Then I notice a black book lying on my desk. The moleskin journal I once gave you. Out of respect for your privacy, I don't read your notebooks, but this time I pick it up. The worn pages reveal leaf after leaf of scribbled poetry. All love poems to Amanda.

From: 'Robyn'
To: 'Stuart'
Sent: 02 February 2006 11:01 AM

My heart inside my chest is struggling to breathe. I read your poems in the black book you left by my computer. It will be good for you to sort out your thoughts.

I will be here, putting one foot in front of the other and trying to pick my hands up on the end of my arms to do the things they are meant to do.

I will smile, I will be a mom, I will help you move…

A few phone calls later, I find a half-finished garden room for you to move into temporarily. I manage to get through the afternoon by obsessively cleaning the dusty room. Retracing my steps, I methodically carry your guitar, then the mattress, kettle, computer, and a few other odds and ends that I bring from home. Arranging and re-arranging them to find that nothing looks quite right. I've become super human, despite the heat. Durban is intolerably humid during the month of February. The physical strength I display contradicts my fragile core. It was only yesterday morning when I cleaned our own home, comfortably sure of my day. Before the words.

This room is reminiscent of the small garden cottage you lived in the first night I came home with you, over eight years ago. Only, this is the end and that was the beginning.

It was a warm Monday night in the late South African spring of 1997 when I first laid eyes on you. My twenty-seven-year-old bones were worn out from working as a secretary during the day and a waitress all evening. The poetry reading was finished by the time I arrived at Bean Bag Bohemia, a trendy bar in the old part of Durban. As I joined a group of friends, a wet nose brushing against my hand from under the table took me by surprise. Two large brown canine eyes peered up at me. It was love-at-first-sight. Above the rim of my coffee cup, I observed with keen interest as the dog identified its owner. You wore a faded T-shirt with beaten-up black jeans and earthy leather boots. A bush of woolly blond curls framed your high forehead above a pair of immense blue eyes. Before we had the opportunity to talk, you left with your lovely reddish-brown three-legged German Pointer bouncing faithfully behind. Feigning casual interest, I found out from my friends that your name was Stuart and that you'd be at their house party that coming Friday night. Picking up on my eagerness, they felt obligated to advise me against getting involved with you. "He's a wild horse," they warned which only served to pique my curiosity.

I arrived late that Friday, dressed in my favorite hippie floral pants and taller than usual in platform shoes. Black curls hung loosely down my back. I spotted you ensconced near the bar with your back pressed against the wall, alone and drinking a beer. You were not extraordinarily tall, but more solid than most at almost six feet. You looked Viking-like, with ruddy English skin and a prominent nose, and I imagined that you would survive war and disease well. A blue work shirt bunched uncomfortably around your shoulders. You emitted a strong male presence in the room; nothing uncertain, nothing vague. I gave you a generous grin; a smile you vowed later you'd never forget. Walking determinedly towards the bar, I introduced myself. For the rest of the night, you were intensely focused on me and I reveled in your attention. The people around seemed to melt away. I sensed a depth in you that was rare. After the party, you offered me a lift home and in the car you turned to me and asked matter-of-factly, "Can I sleep in your hair?" We arrived at your garden cottage and after warily drinking coffee we fell into intoxicated sleep on your single bed; both of us still fully dressed. Breathing gently on my arm beside us, slept your three-legged dog, Mr. Spooks.

I kept the story that you wrote about that night and mailed to a group of friends, months later.

From: 'Stuart'
To: 'Robyn'
Sent: 12 May 1998 02:32 AM

I met her one evening in the most ordinary of environs. There was no smoke in the sky, nor cars parked in uncomfortable positions in the car park. People were mixing affably around the pool and I felt completely alone amongst such real and complacent souls. There were wives and pilots, small-bit heroes and grandiose persons of inflated importance. Their smell of sex stank through their clothing and there was no one but me to be offended by it. Somehow, she singled me out and told me I was the only true person there; that she too was alienated from the chitter and the chatter of other people's lives as they themselves were subject to their own devices.

She was thin, dark haired and had beautifully pointed teeth, her eyes were as clear as my mother's were as I recall her scoldings for things that occurred around the kitchen table. She talked and I drank.

All her words were filled with hard relevance to my despairing position and I listened intently. She would find corners of refuge and turn them over until these bastions of refuge were public between us. She would speak of her fears as if they were my own and I would find myself watching her dark eyes and moist mouth moving as she expressed what I could not. I would nod foolishly at the remarks she made on topics of faith, sex, society, and deeper untold stories of the unspoken heart and I fell headlong into the twisted heart of the lights that burned in her city; all the information, the compassion, the understanding certain women possess; but she was not of any category. I collapsed into her arms as pure relief from my tormented thoughts, thinking: "Here I will find a glass-cut glacier, a water-shed woman built for ice-picks and fires by the candles melting romance into songs from moist lips and extravagant approvals."

I split my desires in two – one: the giving – the softest touch to a sleeping brow; the kiss on unopened lips, the other… the other! Speak to me! Let me hear how foul I have become. Let me hear from your mouth how I am! Show me in real actions how I can re-arrange myself to be a man compatible with another woman!

All these things she understands, although when I speak of darker things, her eyes move with mine – truth will lie alongside the most beautiful music and fatal road accidents simultaneously. How I was supposed to express my small (but important) affiliation to the joy and beauty of being alive would only live in the realm of childhood imagination.

Now it's late and I'm faced with an angel that comes from good cooking, distant city lights, and sex taken softly and words... words... Her words spin my melancholy into remorse; all my life I've needed truth, and beneath dark eyebrows my concentration falters – I love her for this and I ask her "can I sleep in your hair?" She agrees and her hair becomes her body. Slender thighs and softly lit bedroom lights...

I am sucked back into the present when you arrive home after what you describe as an unbearable day at work. I watch you pack a small backpack of clothes. Following you around aimlessly, I attempt to make myself useful by spluttering out directions to your new spot. Food is out of the question, and even the wine tastes bland. You leave abruptly. I listen to the noise of your motorbike fade away into the far distance, until all I can hear is the beating of my own heart. I am alone.

Sitting on the paved stairway leading down into our garden, I roll my first cigarette in two years. From here I have an ideal view of our house. My house. It is as beautiful as it was the moment we first saw it.

I remember the dull day at work in mid-1998, eight months into our dating. You rescued me from the office to go and have a look at a house that was for sale. Large trees lined the streets of the arty suburb near the university. The sunken property was hidden from view by a wild flowering bougainvillea hedge. We opened the garden gate and peered down a long brick stairway, lined with clusters of bamboo, at the quaint green wood-and-iron farmhouse. Instantly we both knew that we had to own it. We borrowed money and signed the papers to purchase the house two days later.

This tobacco is old. It may even be two years old and I've forgotten how to roll cigarettes. In desperation, I manage somehow. I feel nauseous; although I'm not sure the sick feeling is from the nicotine. Through the smoke, I remember the times we sat on these stairs together. How some nights you would come home late and, missing you in bed, I'd find you out here; smoking cigarettes and staring at the house. We'd sit together, nestled in our lush garden with elephant ears, palm trees, and bamboo extending like tender fingers holding our beloved home. We knew we were lucky to have found it.

The house seems so empty now. I feel utterly alone. What will I tell the girls? I sit in the darkness for a long time. Tiny ants crowd around me. I barely notice. I just sit. I smoke. In utter disbelief and despair. Perhaps I am waiting to be tired enough to go to sleep. Perhaps I'm hoping that I am asleep, and I will soon awaken from this nightmare. When I curl up into bed alone, I draw your pillow towards me, and then I see the saddest thing. Your wrinkled sleeping shorts are still under your pillow. I clutch them against me and weep until I feel as though my lungs are being torn from my chest.

3

The garden room you are staying in is ten minutes drive from our house. During the week the girls are away, I visit you with dinner and wine each night. The dinner remains untouched. Food seems irrelevant, and I can't bring myself to put so much as a morsel near my mouth. The musty room is only five broad steps in length and three in width. A single mattress lies on the cement floor. Your guitar balances in a corner next to a cardboard box holding the computer. Between your room and the bathroom is a covered concrete slab. Two teacups, a kettle, and some tea bags perch on top of the outside fridge. The fridge is bare except for a carton of milk and two beer quarts.

We sit on the hard concrete floor and drink wine out of teacups while talking by candlelight. I ask the questions, trying to make sense of it all.

"Stu…" I venture into uncertain territory, "Why didn't you just tell me earlier? I could've… we could've maybe –"

"I dunno," you say sorrowfully. "I wanted to, but I just kept hoping to get out of this mess myself without having to bring you into it."

Bleakness permeates the moist air and seeps into my pores. Don't cry, I tell myself sternly. If I break down in front of you, it will be unlikely that you will continue to talk. Inside I am emptier than the fridge, but I sit dry-eyed, taking in each piece of information. I keep it together partly because I am still in shock but mainly because I crave more details. My confidence disintegrates listening to your tortured sobs as you reveal everything.

You admit that you kept hoping that you would be able to get over Amanda and move on; knowing how many people it would hurt if you couldn't. I learn that it was love-at-first-sight for both of you. A mutual emotional relationship that up until this point has not been physical.

"We haven't had sex," you somberly declare. "It's been unbearable… having her so near, smelling her skin, wanting to touch her. The heat when we are close… but it would cause too much damage. I never wanted to hurt you, you know."

I give a slight humph and swallow hard. It is a small but uncomforting relief to find out that you have not slept with her,

14

that she has not claimed you entirely. As your story continues, though, I begin to understand that although Amanda may not have possessed your body, she has most certainly consumed the rest of you.

Following these conversations, I go home and sit on the shadowy stairway where I smoke cigarette after cigarette. Then I come back the next night for more. I need to figure out the whole puzzle, to try and fit together all the pieces in order to work out how this could happen to us. I never thought it would.

It was barely a week after buying the house when the topic of marriage came up. We were driving up to Johannesburg where you had a work function and we were to visit my parents.

Sometime during the six-hour journey you said, "I love you completely and I would do anything for you. Marry you if that's what you want."

"How does the end of September sound?" was my eager reply.

Two months afterwards, I sat grinning in the stark courtroom in a simple blue dress, holding the colorful spring posy that your mom picked from her garden. Our families gathered round while *Moon River* whined out from a friend's violin. We exchanged rings, kissed and signed papers. Before I knew it, we were married.

Your family and friends seemed to sigh with relief at the idea that you had finally settled down. My parents, on the other hand, kept their thoughts to themselves but I sensed that they were disappointed. They had dreams for me, as all parents do, that I would marry a homely and stable man. But I didn't want a boring, sugary and predictable life. I wanted adventure, risk and romance. I had never met anyone quite as impulsive or romantic as you before or anyone who loved me so entirely. There was a wildness about you, something untamed, yet gentle as the autumn breeze. Some thought that I might finally be the one to tame you. But your character could not be contained. Neither did I try.

After we were married, I quit my job as a secretary and continued to work as a waitress at night. You sold books for a living, although your passion lay in music and writing. I was in awe of your talent as a composer, songwriter, guitar and piano player as well as your ability to write prize-winning poetry and off-beat short stories. You were the most unusual and creative person I had ever met.

Your keen penchant for excess went beyond your drinking. You threw yourself into every task with a zeal and passion that I admired, whether it was painting the walls or swimming lengths in the public pool each morning. Almost everything you did was extreme. You were larger than life with boundless energy. Nothing was dull with you around.

The two of us were rebels in our own right, swimming upstream, against the current of society. I was the type of person who loved conspiracy theories and anything else that challenged one's truth or beliefs. Neither of us was fond of mediocrity.

In those early days we'd lie in bed and smoke cigarettes with a glass of red wine while you'd read to me from classic romance novels or play the guitar and sing. Mr. Spooks always lay with us; he was a part of you. Often we would play card games or scrabble long into the night. Some nights after waitressing, I'd come and watch you playing music, a mixture of edgy rock, blues and good-time jazz in dingy pubs around the city. On stage, you excelled. Before an audience is where you were at your best. On occasion, you would stand up on a chair and shout out to no one in particular, "This is my wife. Isn't she beautiful?"

You used to assure me that all we'd ever need was each other. Falling asleep on top of you, I knew that I was made just for that place. Your arms wrapped around me, and we fitted together perfectly. Pulling me nearer you would murmur that it was not close enough for you; that you wanted to unzip my skin and climb inside me, so we could be even closer. Be one.

One day I confided in a friend, that my greatest fear was a feeling I had that you would not be around forever. It seemed to me that your light shone too brightly, and so much vigor couldn't possibly last.

And now as we sit outside your garden room, I listen to your dreams of having a life together with Amanda. You grumble that you have left your family for her, yet she shows no sign of doing the same. Complaining that you have nothing to hold onto at night but your pillow, still, you are convinced that she will come. I argue that she will not follow through, but you refuse to hear it. Insisting that what you have is different; special. A love that is not of this world. I stare out into the muggy darkness as you speak. The bushes seem to be ominous black creatures threatening to come and get me. I almost wish they were; although there's not much left for them to take.

I decide to contact Barry and learn that Amanda has not mentioned anything about the relationship to him. So I relay what I have discovered and he listens in disbelief. Barry is convinced that it is a one-sided romance and that Amanda does not reciprocate your feelings, although he admits that she has become withdrawn.

As the days go on, you grow deeply depressed. I am reminded of the story you told me of the agonizing separation between you and your ex-girlfriend Melissa before we met. She left you one spectacular spring afternoon for another man. You admitted to spending many nights pitifully lying on wet leaves outside her bedroom window weeping and begging. It took you over a year to surface again. I can't help but wonder. How long will it take you this time?

4

I am anxious about fetching Jane and Rose from the airport, terrified of bringing them home to a place where you no longer live. They do not know. My mother is with them and will be staying with us for a couple of days. Her presence should provide a welcome distraction for the girls and what is missing at home. I look forward to seeing them. I also feel sick. I'm still not sure what I will tell them.

Returning from the airport, I hold my breath as they happily run through the house. They don't notice that anything is amiss. I breathe out. As casually as I can muster, I explain that you have been working especially hard and that there is so much to do that you will have to sleep at work for a while. I let them know that you won't be coming home tonight. The excitement of being home seems to override this news. After voicing their disappointment, they head off to play with much-missed toys.

However, you do wind up popping in to see them on your way home from work. Jane and Rose sprint up the stairs to greet you. As you swoop them both up in your arms, I can see your eyes over the top of their hair. They are frightened, sad eyes. I smile and keep moving, putting on a brave face and doing my best to be normal. I act as if everything is going to be alright and deep down, I do believe this. All looks as it should on the outside.

After a brief visit, you are gone again. Snuggling into bed with the girls, I read them a bedtime story. It is not a sad story, but I have to swallow my tears, when the little rabbit can't find his home. Tomorrow I'll have to choose more carefully. I sing them the same lullaby I've sang for years and then lie still until I detect their steady breathing. Only then do I dare to look at them. I stare at Jane and Rose's sleeping faces and close my hand over my mouth to stifle a sob. Why aren't you here? You love these two girls more than anything. Tonight you won't be able to kiss their foreheads, or wrap your arms around Rose all night as she wriggles and nuzzles closer to you. Usually you and Rose share one half of the king-size bed and Jane and I, the other. Now I look at innocence on either side of a huge space. Empty. Waiting for you. Looking at them takes me back six years to a night we were at a party.

We had been married for around five months and had both discussed wanting children. Without warning, you casually announced to the group sitting on the grass that you were going to go for a vasectomy. Hoping my face did not reveal the shock, I silently reminded myself to remain calm. This was how you did things. Loathing polite conversation, you often made a point of being controversial and opinionated, blurting out what was not generally considered acceptable in polite company. You proffered a position intended to piss others off and scrutinize their vulnerability. Pushing buttons and boundaries was your way of prodding and challenging the very meaning of existence. You did this without consideration of the consequences, laughing off the cruelty on the beer or the bourbon or whatever drink was being offered at the time. I understood all this, and it hardly ever fazed me. Except when you were really hurtful to people and I had to apologize for your behavior.

When the two of us were at home, I broached the subject. You ran out of the room crying. I found you curled up in a fetal position on the bathroom floor.

"You don't understand," you blurted out, "I can't have children."

"Shhh, shhh…" I consoled, wondering what on earth you were talking about.

"The world is too scary. It wouldn't be right to bring another human being here."

I rubbed your back.

"It's not fair to give anyone my genes or for anyone to have to be like me. To feel like I do or to see what I see. I can't do that to anyone."

This all took me completely by surprise. I comforted you. I held you like the children I feared I would now never have. I rocked you and stroked your hair and took you to bed. The following morning you apologized and confirmed that you did want children. I was relieved but confused.

On occasions such as these, I caught glimpses of your dark, muddy bits. The inner self you had warned me about. They would surface temporarily and you said things you'd later disown, things as if spoken by another. Not the man I believed you to be, the one I had come to adore.

A year after that night, on your 32nd birthday, January 26th 2000, I discovered that I was pregnant. Knowing by this time you would also be thrilled, I wrapped up the positive test stick and left the package on your pillow as a birthday gift. When you found it, you behaved like an overly excitable boy.

I worked as a waitress until I was seven months pregnant. Once I finally quit it was difficult surviving without my wages, but we were content with our basic lifestyle. We started a small business from home, a music recording studio in the building at the bottom of the garden.

The moment our first daughter, Jane, was born you were the happiest and proudest I had ever seen you. You were a hands-on dad right from the beginning, eagerly helping with night-time feedings, baths and diaper changes. Although I could no longer join you on nights out, you and Mr. Spooks would go out together. When you'd get home, you always poked your head into the bedroom and said, "Hello my darlings!" No matter what time it happened to be, I got out of bed and joined you for a coffee and cigarette to listen to your stories. You would transport me to the scenes and landscapes of your world through your tales. The people or places that most folk avoided were the ones that fascinated you. You did not accept societal stereotypes of race, class, gender and income, preferring to make up your own. You felt comfortable with the underdog, the misunderstood, and those on the margin. Your heart was as wide open as the ocean. Sometimes you would bring home tramps and prostitutes for a cup of tea and a safe bed. One bright morning as I got into the car, I found a red high-heel shoe on the floor. We laughed afterwards about the hooker you offered a lift, leaving her one shoe behind.

In March 2002, we were ecstatic to have another baby girl, Rose. You never wanted sons. Perhaps you didn't see daughters as being too similar to yourself. Having a young baby and a toddler was tiring for me but you were an enormous help, fully present and involved while you were at home. You leapt into the task of fatherhood with the same enthusiasm you had for your music. Despite being at work all day, you came home and did the cooking and dishwashing. After bathing and dressing the girls, you would be the one to read them bedtime stories, giving me a break to catch up on e-mail or administration. We usually had a drink together before you went down to the studio to compose and record music or went out on your own. In this way, I hardly noticed your absence on the nights you were out.

I started getting up less and less when you came home late, and much of your drinking during this time passed me by. While others complained of hangovers, you were oddly at your best the morning after. Somehow still able to get up early, you would go to the beach or the pool for a swim before we were awake. Then you came home to tend to the girls and bring me coffee in bed with a familiar sweet, stale yeasty smell oozing out of your pores; a smell I associated with your good mood. On weekends, you'd take the girls to the beach or the park with Mr. Spooks to give me time off. We all slept cuddled up in one loving family bed. Of all your talents, the one that I thought you were finest at was being an extraordinary dad.

Our home was your place of safety in an intimidating world. Many people knew nothing of your home life, and were surprised to find out that you had a family. You kept it close to you like a precious belonging. This house, our home. Your three girls, you claimed, were the best things that ever happened to you.

Letter August 2002

Sweetest of hearts –

Just because I may not always say how much I love you doesn't mean I don't –

I've never been this happy in my whole life. Just sitting on the steps last night looking at our house and knowing that, inside there, somewhere, are these two little girls and one big one all sleeping under the same roof as me is such a delight.

What can(!) I say! Thank you. Thank you for being on this weird and wonderful planet with me – I love you more than I love my dearest thoughts.

Your 'usband
Stuart

5

Happy days and months turned into years. In mid 2003, an opportunity arose for you to head up a new jazz band. I encouraged this even though it meant weeks of rehearsals and more nights out. I had always supported your creative endeavors, as you seemed to be more fulfilled when you had one in the works.

You were not a depressive person but you experienced sporadic down times. Weeks of space where you were not as alive as you could be; where the colours of your world seemed to fade to gray. Everything seemed to affect you more deeply than the average person. It was almost as if you lacked the filters that most of us keep in place for our own protection. Instead, you took the whole lot in and this resulted in your viewing the world on some days as a beautiful and mystifying place, and on others, as a rotting and vile hell full of misery and danger. I noticed that this dismal outlook often occurred when you lacked a creative outlet. The slumps of gloom ended when the next project started forming in your mind, the next story or song.

At the opening concert of your new band, I met the singer who sang alongside you, for the first time. Her name was Amanda. Afterwards, the three of us had drinks with the rest of the band. You were shining.

That year things started to change. At first I was barely aware of it. A slow transition. I made excuses for everything, convincing myself that this is how it goes in marriage. Not every day can be blissful. You seemed to grow dimmer; fading away from me with the passing months. Your bouts of despondency began to go on longer than they used to and became more regular. I had no idea that this had anything to do with another woman.

Life at home continued to be accompanied by the soundtrack of your guitar. "Make your sickness your art," you said. Losing yourself in the music you became one with the tempo, swooping and bowing, your flat fingers forming complex rhythms reminiscent of Django Reinhardt, until the world around you faded, and only the music existed.

You were given a piano accordion and for a while, our soundtrack changed. The wheezing and whining of your practicing filled the garden, and you learned the instrument quickly. The accordion now accompanied you and Mr. Spooks down to the harbor at night where you sat at the docks, drinking quart beers and practicing to the silhouettes of ships and sailors.

When you came home in the dead of the night, I started getting up to meet you again as the girls grew older. At times, you would still speak of the world as a mysterious place, full of beauty and sorrow. But then there were nights that you would squint and a frown furrowed deep between your eyebrows. On these occasions, I knew not to stay up too long. It wasn't that we fought, but you began to criticize me as part of the *fridge-world*. This was the name you gave to the parts of humanity that you hated, describing them as dangerous, dark and cold. Your fridge-world, this world you despised, was made up of the things that most people viewed as normal.

In the mornings following nights such as these, while drinking tea and playing your guitar on the veranda, you would turn to me and sing an old jazz standard.

You always hurt, the one you love,
the one you shouldn't hurt at all.
You always take the sweetest rose,
and crush it, till the petals fall.
You always break the kindest heart,
with a hasty word that you can't recall.
So if I broke your heart last night,
it's because I love you most of all.

In June of 2004, your long-time canine friend and your shadow in the world, Mr. Spooks, died. At fourteen years old, his one arthritic front leg could no longer carry him. After two weeks of seeing him unable to walk at all, you had to make the unbearable decision to end his suffering. Sitting with him at the vet, you stroked his old nose, sobbing while the lethal injection slowly put him to sleep.

Mr. Spooks had walked a long way with you from your distant hippie days when you lived in a country commune. He was the soft nuzzle of comfort, the faithful audience at all your music gigs, your strong swimming partner in the sea and the patient companion on all your late night jaunts into the inner city bars and to the docks. Together you would howl at the full moon and sit arm in paw, watching the world go by. You felt that Mr. Spooks understood you like no one else ever could. He instinctively knew how to comfort you when you were down. You would pull him to you and curl around his doggie frame and, somehow, Spooks could take away the pain. Mr. Spooks was no ordinary dog.

The girls and I were devastated too. Mr. Spooks had been a part of our family. At our wedding, he was your best man and proudly wore a doggie cravat.

Mr. Spooks had a nervous nibble. In a situation where he felt uncomfortable, he would start nibbling his one remaining front paw. He had the softest coat and was the best afternoon snoozing partner on a rainy day. When Jane was a baby, I would discover her giggling, lying next to Mr. Spooks in his large basket. Rose, the messier of our two babies, would happily sit and eat Spooks' food with him out of his bowl as soon as she was able to crawl. A German Pointer, Spooks was a hunter by breed. You couldn't mention the word 'rat' around him without having him go into seek-and-destroy mode with a fanatical intensity. Once while out with you, Spooks had gnawed and scratched with his one front paw, nearly through a wooden bar counter, searching for the elusive rodent. In our wooden house, 'rat' was a forbidden word, even as a joke.

After Mr. Spooks was gone, you spoke more of the fridge-world. At the end of that year, you quit selling books, saying you were tired of jobbing and preferred to stay at home to write and play music gigs to make money. Pleased about a creative move, I ignored the reality of the financial hardship this might bring because I sensed it would make you happier.

We fixed up a tiny room outside the house as a space where you could start writing the novel that had been taking form in your head. We had both quit smoking by this time, but you started smoking again. Your evenings were spent in the writing room, drinking whiskey, puffing on cigarettes and putting your ideas to paper. I silently retreated to the comfort of my own computer doing research, writing, and web design. We took breaks together discussing our work. Afterwards we would head to our room to join our sleeping girls in bed.

We spoke of our dreams of moving to the country, a life perfectly suited to two idealists. You could have your own writing room and I could grow my herbs. We got excited about the idea of sustainable living and a place where our girls could grow up freely, just as you did on a farm. I imagined we would be happier in the country with less of the darkness of the city to bring you down. You perked up and I was thrilled to notice that your old contented self made a re-appearance.

We lived with the money shortage for a while, but soon you accepted a part-time job at the newspaper where Ruth worked. Your sister Ruth and you had stood steadfastly together from childhood; guarding each other intensely. Whenever the world was too crushing, you had each other. Shortly after starting your new job, Ruth moved to Cape Town with her husband, Bradley.

I felt you slipping away. I scrambled to bring you back. I tried to think of when you first started drifting. I couldn't put my finger on it. It was just that, in the first few years together, you were kind. Before you would leave home in the morning, you'd come into the room and bring me coffee. Sitting down gently on the bed, you'd wake me up with small kisses on my forehead and whisper "Morning my love." I'd gaze up into your transparent blue eyes smiling down at me. You'd stroke my hair and smell my hairline; a scent you believed could reveal everything about someone's essence. It's those things I remember. When we were out and socializing, you'd keep those eyes on me. They'd smile and dance and question to see if I was all right. I'd know wherever you were across the room from the love that beamed from those eyes. As the years went by, I began to see it less and less. Lately, you still made me coffee every morning. But I woke up to the smell of it next to my bed and the hum of your motorbike leaving. I noticed all this, but put it down to the way things go. I missed it. I longed for it to return, this warmth. I was sure it would. But instead it became even less frequent. When we were out, I searched for your eyes across the room but couldn't find them. I felt ignored. Sometimes, I felt as if it didn't matter to you whether I was here or not. I felt invisible.

Although we had always maintained our own groups of

friends, I began seeing less of mine. In an effort to hold my family together, I spent more time at home trying to be the perfect wife. I began to seek out meaning in my life, exclusive of you. I started visiting a Buddhist retreat center, listening to inspirational talks, and reading self-help books. Buddha advises one to stop looking outside for happiness and rather to look within. I meditated and searched and found that although I was mostly happy, this didn't change a feeling I had that you didn't love me like you used to do.

One night, I came down to the recording studio where you were working. I stood behind you for a while until you turned around to glance at me. I asked if you loved me. You stopped working and leaned closer as if noticing me for the first time in weeks. You had a strange look on your face that I couldn't quite place. My tears came from nowhere. "Do you love me Stuart?" I asked again. You stopped what you were doing, walked me back up to the veranda, sat down and sighed.

"Yes, Robyn, of course I love you." But that was all you offered me, and I couldn't see any emotion in your eyes. In your voice, I heard no certainty; no reassurance. I cried harder. You held me, but your arms didn't have the life they used to have. I wanted to believe you. But your attention seemed elsewhere. No longer did you speak of climbing into my skin. There was no more standing up on chairs to declare your love for me. Perhaps that is what happened when a couple had been together for years. After all, romance changes with time.

On our seventh wedding anniversary, I wrote a poem and folded it up in a paper airplane on your pillow. You made no comment on it, and the airplane lay next to the bed for a week until I retrieved it and kept it. I still had the wrinkled poem in my handbag four months later, when I found out you were in love with Amanda. When I heard the words.

Seven Years

On the veranda in years to come,
I will look across at your whiskey nose
and I will love that nose, the creases,
the bumps, the grooves...
I will hear the creak of the rocking chair
your rhythmic back and forth
moon madness will shine in your eyes,
I will love those eyes, blue turned to gray,
in between, frown lines from years of pondering,
on the side, sleep lines from years of tossing
I will trace your face in my mind,
staring at the man I love, the man I will always love...

Robyn – Sept 2005

6

You don't last long in that garden room you moved into the day after I found out you were in love with Amanda. After three weeks, you ask to move home until you can find a more suitable place. I agree hastily; sure that once you are here, we will have another chance. You will remember that we are a family.

It becomes increasingly clear however, that this is not to be. On the mornings I wake up early, I catch you crying. I make extra effort to keep the days busy and enjoyable for the girls. In the afternoons when you come home from work, you and I drink coffee on the veranda and you jabber about your day. Mostly, you talk of Amanda. There are more tears. I keep this well hidden from the girls by letting them watch countless movies to keep occupied. I am fiercely protective over their happiness. At dinners, I barely touch my food. You make an attempt to appear light-hearted around the girls and still tuck them into bed. Once they are asleep, we sit on the veranda some more and drink. By now, almost everything you say relates to her. Nothing else seems to matter to you anymore. It is dreadfully apparent that you are not emotionally stable. I cautiously suggest that you visit a therapist to get a handle on your sorrow but you refuse as I suspect you will. As much as I want to fall apart, I have to be the steady one. I want you to keep talking to me for your own sake rather than mine. Then too, I have a feeling that the more you talk, the more I will know where I stand and how I might make this all better. As you speak, my rational mind works to find solutions.

Barry and I start communicating on the phone daily. He has plenty of questions and acknowledges that Amanda is miserable. I find myself being stretched back and forth between phone calls with Barry and conversations with you. I am aware of where my loyalties lie. Keeping Amanda and Barry's marriage together is clearly to my advantage. I meet his questions as best I can but continually urge him to seek the truth from his wife. Barry confirms that Amanda has admitted to loving you, but I'm not sure that she offers him much else. I assume this from hearing two different versions of the story each day.

There is no moon tonight and summer rain falls like sheets of glass off the tin roof and down the sides of the veranda. Music penetrates the soupy air and loops around me. You sit across from me in your rocking chair listening to the latest mix of sentimental love songs from your new album. Words of love and loss; slow and sad. Words you wrote for her. I am choked by thoughts of what could have been. The girls are curled up obliviously in bed and one of our dogs lies at my feet as if she can sense my devastation. You rock and lament about how you can't live and breathe without her and I sit here feeling the same about you. You tell me that you are only home until you find somewhere else to go. Somewhere she can come to you. You still hold hope that she is coming.

You join the girls in bed and I stay on the veranda. My feet are curled underneath me on an old sunken cushion. In the glow from the yellow garden light overhead, I watch my cigarette smoke coil and disappear, curl and vanish, concentrating on the unique patterns that are forming. For a fleeting time there is nothing else on my mind except this image. Just a brief moment of oblivion before the feelings take over. The sense that I cannot breathe has nothing to do with the two boxes of cigarettes I have already inhaled today. A gnome stares at me from the green shrubbery across the garden and my deep love for this house makes the tragedy more painful. Seven years of affection witnessed now only by the collection of clutter, each piece with its own memory. I consider running away and taking the girls with me. But I can't leave this house. I can't leave you. I think of Mr. Spooks. If only he was here now. He would lie with you, and you could cry into the folds of his old doggie shoulder. I suddenly miss him more than I ever have.

I had a dream, as a young child – a house and a white fence similar to the one trailing around the veranda with jasmine, and a garden full of herbs and children playing merrily. In this dream there was someone who would love me. We would grow old together, sitting and laughing in the chairs where I now sit alone.

Earlier this evening, as we sat outside huddled from the rain, you talked about your childhood. Telling me of a promise that you made when you were seven years old; a pact you intended to keep. "What promise?" I asked. You wouldn't elaborate. It was a sacred contract. As you spoke, I pictured a young boy, all scruffy clothes and wavy hair; bright eyed and eager. A child who felt the need to make this promise to himself. I questioned what brought you to that point and you admitted that you didn't know. You couldn't remember a trauma; unable to recall much before that age. You grappled for reasons as to why you are so screwed up, but you could not find any. It seemed that even at the tender age of seven, you had already decided the world was a scary place, not to be trusted.

PART II

7

Exactly one month has passed since I heard the words. The girls and I wait at the airport for our two-hour flight to Cape Town to visit your sister Ruth and her husband Bradley; a trip that was booked a while ago. To minimize your time off work, you will join us in three days. I buy a journal at the bookshop to write down my thoughts; a safe place to express myself. There's an hour wait before takeoff. I stare out the towering glass windows at the planes flying overhead, silver wings cutting across the infinite gray sky. Jane and Rose play happily, seeing an exciting holiday ahead. They have no concept of the inconceivable events of the past month or of the weight that travels with me.

The narrow veranda in front of Ruth and Bradley's Cape Town house is bordered by a white slatted wooden fence. Ruth and I sit chatting and sipping on Merlot. Ruth is the female version of you in a number of ways, with short cropped blond hair and the same piercing blue eyes. She has a similar nervousness about the world but has managed to transform it through responsibility and achievement. Warm and gentle, Ruth is the best comrade you could have wished for in a sibling. The girls and I adore her.

At midnight, the shrill ring of my cell phone confirms my suspicions as I see your name displayed on the tiny screen.

There's a strange coolness in your voice when you inform me that you have decided to go camping in the mountains for the week, instead of joining us as planned. I shift in my seat, unsettled, while Ruth stares at me above the rim of her glass. You will leave right away, drive through the night and will not be taking your cell phone. Even though I can tell that it's pointless to convince you otherwise, I make a feeble effort nonetheless. You cut me short and end by affirming that you love me and insisting that I must look after the girls.

I think of you riding alone towards the bitter mountain air, your tiny motorbike in the vast darkness. Ruth and I stay up late and finish off another bottle of wine. Tomorrow I will break the news to Jane and Rose. I don't look forward to it. They were barely able to fall asleep tonight; so excited for your arrival tomorrow. But I figure that I can say you have too much work again.

A phone call from Beverley interrupts our mutual hangover early the next morning. Beverley is an artist in every sense of the word and one of your closest friends. Having once dated, your sincere friendship has eclipsed the former feelings. She is one of the people who get you. I watch Ruth's face as she listens to what Beverley has to say and I know that it is not good news.

"Beverley was with Stuart last night," Ruth tells me, "He told her his plan and asked her not to tell anyone." I swig my last sip of coffee and wait for her to go on.

"She said that he was alarmingly calm when he explained that he was going to the mountains for a week. He was going to ask Amanda to join him there. If she doesn't arrive then he knows that there is no point in living and doesn't plan on coming home."

Stunned, I follow Ruth to the kitchen where she puts on the kettle again as she gravely continues. "Beverley tried to talk some sense into him; she pleaded and begged him to think about his family, his children. But he didn't want to hear any of it. So she left in anger after telling him that she wanted no part in his plan."

Ruth and I sit down in the sun outside with our mugs of steaming coffee in a bewildered panic.

"What should we do?" I ask.

"I don't know," Ruth says, "Beverley has already phoned Amanda and she was just as shocked. Stuart sent her a message to tell her where he is. He didn't mention anything about a time limit or his plan to Amanda though. Beverley told Amanda that part."

"So when is Amanda going?"

"It doesn't sound like she is from what Beverley gathered. She said she has rehearsals all week."

Without your cell phone, Ruth and I have no way of reaching you and we are a thousand miles away. I suddenly think about the two long, white scars running up from your wrists; souvenirs from your army days. You were young, only eighteen years old and although you never talked about the details, I understood that the army was an extremely traumatic time for you. I assumed that when I met you, you were long past your suicidal days. Could I have been that wrong?

Phone calls go back and forth as we all plead with Amanda. No one shows any signs of coming to your rescue. Barry tries to convince me that it is only manipulation, an empty threat. Ruth and I aren't prepared to take that chance. I want to scream; to shout out that a life is on the line. My husband's life. The man I love. Isn't anyone listening? The father of our two girls. My pleas fall on deaf ears. The days that follow are an excruciating waiting game. Ruth and I make an effort to do fun things with the girls while we quietly live through a nightmare.

We are surrounded by crystals. Jane and Rose are collecting them at the Scratch Patch at the Cape Town Waterfront. Ruth sits across from me. We share the same fear. It is inscribed on our faces, a look we both recognize in each other.

The days blur into each other; a parade of shops, sea, wine, and cigarettes. And worry. Dread. My nails dig into the flesh of my hands while I sleep and I wake up with my tense jaw aching. Time is running out. My mind doesn't rest. I keep phoning Amanda and Barry, like a stalker. She hasn't gone yet? She can't get out of rehearsals. Barry won't let her go. It is not her fault but I am fuming.

On day six, I can't risk it any longer. We change our tickets and fly home a day earlier than planned. Racing. The plane touches down in Durban. I can still get to you in time. Amanda has let me know where you are. What will you do when I come? Will I be enough to save you? One last phone call. I call Amanda and Barry. Barry agrees to let her come to you at last. I pray that she will make it on time. Am I doing the right thing? There is one day left. While Amanda drives up to the mountains to find you, Barry and I stay awake all night on our veranda waiting, drinking, talking, and passing time. As it turns out, we had reason to worry; but a reason less terrifying than death.

Amanda phones in the morning to say that you are on your way back to Durban. I am so relieved that I even manage to thank her. As your motorbike pulls into the driveway, the girls and I run up to greet you. In that moment, nothing else matters. You are home.

That night when the girls are fast asleep, you tell me that you and Amanda sat on a wooden bridge with your legs swinging back and forth talking for hours, until you fell drunk into your tiny tent and had sex for the first time. I sit calmly and say that it's fine. I'm fine. With a disgusted frown, you ask me how I can sit here and tell you that it is alright. Don't I want to shout and express how much I hate you? No. I sit quietly. I wanted to shout and scream to save your life, but not now. I can't. All I can tell you is that it's okay. I love you. You shake your head and hate yourself even more. You will never know what I've been through this last week. How the only important thing to me was to see you again, alive. You could have said anything and it would've been alright with me. You are here, you are still here.

8

I first met Amanda at the opening performance of your new jazz band in 2003. I sat tall and proud, listening to you singing together. You had spoken of her often during the weeks of rehearsals, relaying stories of helping with her young baby that was constantly on her hip. Amanda was curvaceous with startlingly large green eyes set off by skin the color of toffee. Her long dark hair hung in perfectly coiled ringlets and her smile seemed genuine enough. She moved like a cat, graceful yet jumpy. I observed her carefully.

The concert was such a success that soon preparations were underway for a second performance. Eventually, the band began travelling to different cities to perform. During this time, you developed a close friendship with Amanda that continued even once the band had broken up a year later; meeting for cappuccinos and sending each other text messages regularly. You had always had female friends and I had never felt threatened by them in any way. This time was no different to me. Slowly, Amanda and I became friends. Our children got on so well that we began to meet regularly for coffee. Soon Jane and Amanda's eldest son had become best friends, enjoying frequent play dates and occasional sleepovers.

One day, roughly two years after that debut concert, a friend called to say that she'd heard rumors going around town about the two of you. I replaced the telephone receiver and took a slow sip of my coffee. Deliberately twisting the wedding ring on my finger, I studied its Celtic design. Amanda was my friend. This couldn't be true. Still, I felt ill. I was trembling when I asked you to tell me the truth. You stared calmly at me, your blue eyes as clear as the ocean and you assured me that it was merely vicious Durban gossip.

That night we met with Amanda and Barry at their house to iron out the situation. Over wine, you both sat and convinced Barry and I that there was no truth in the rumors and no need for concern. The two of you were just friends. The small balcony sank into uncomfortable silence. I didn't know what to think. I watched Amanda closely but couldn't pick up any deceitfulness in her tears. I glanced down at my flavorless wine as if the truth might be found there. I had no choice. I had to trust you. Of course, I trusted you.

Not long afterwards, Amanda approached you with the idea of singing together in an upcoming music festival. Just the two of you. Barry was unhappy with this. I had reservations, but offered you my support. You spent countless cappuccino-fuelled hours writing the songs together followed by weeks of intense rehearsals. All this was done during school holidays and I looked after the four children. Jane was thrilled to spend a good deal of time with her best friend. They had become inseparable.

Our two families celebrated New Year's Eve 2005 together at Amanda and Barry's house. You sat distant and alone at the fire the entire evening. At the strike of twelve, I sadly noticed that you kissed everyone Happy New Year but me.

The music festival took place towards the end of January 2006. Barry and I sat together at both performances. He was not impressed. The love songs were, admittedly, a tad too close for comfort and slightly embarrassing in light of the previous rumors. I held my head high and thought that I was probably over-reacting. Amanda gave you a post-gig gift, somewhat of a tradition. It was a silver flask engraved with her nickname for you. *Norbert.*

It was a week later when Jane and Rose left for their holiday with Barry. That was the day I found out that things would never be the same.

Sitting on the veranda now, you are home but not here. Words keep coming, pouring out of you like a never-ending confession. You get up despondently from the rocking chair and I feel a friendly pat on my shoulder as you leave to go out for the night. From deep within, the sobs creep up and I surrender. Sadness I have carried around for these past two months and for much of the previous two years. I dry my eyes as a sleepy five-year-old Jane wanders towards me. Scooping her up into my arms, I take her back to bed and slip in beside her. Curled between my two girls, the warmth of what remains of my family surrounds me as I enter the nothingness of sleep, my only current escape.

9

Last night a tramp saved your life. You stumble in before dawn and fall into bed but can't sleep. Your tossing and sighing wakes me up and we both just get up and make coffee. It's still dark outside as you describe how you flung yourself into the sea. You say a homeless man pulled you out. I wonder if you are over-dramatizing the story but you look so bleak and bedraggled that I am plagued with worry.

I am beginning to understand that you are not merely down in the dumps about a botched love affair; you are dangerously depressed to the point of being suicidal. I wish this were more about me. It would be simpler that way; if I were just struggling with my own heartache. But I am rational enough to know that I am dealing with a far greater issue. The matter at hand is not one of simply saving a shattered marriage but rather about saving a life.

During the day, Amanda calls to say that she is on her way to the Rob Roy Hotel for two nights. She has told Barry that she needs some alone time. I have no idea how the plans are made between the two of you, but you want to go up and join her for a night. I agree that you should go to her.

The next morning when you come home, you complain that you were too worn-out after your encounter with the sea and that it did not go as well as it should have. You confide that your second opportunity for sex with Amanda was awkward and uncomfortable. I feel a slight sense of satisfaction, but at the same time, I know this is not good.

Much of your inward struggle comes down to an overwhelming confusion for you on two topics that you talk about incessantly. Love and sex. Sex and love. We have gone around and around in circles discussing them until I find myself as confused as you are. I can no longer remember if it is you or I who claim they are inseparable.

For you and I, sex was a dance we did well. The steps flawlessly timed to a song that was always slightly different. In our crisp white cotton sheets, after a long and gentle waltz or a quick and sexy salsa, we would lie clinging and caressing.

Your two chances to explore this with Amanda are disappointing. The excuse is that you were too drunk or too tired. You say it isn't fair; you need more time to explore one another. You long for another chance. You want the dreams you have in your head to become reality. I think about this. Perhaps the illusions will be crushed and shattered the minute you spend some real time together. I mention this to Barry, "Let's throw them together for a month or so with all the kids." A crazy notion, but it may bring the best outcome for all. The imaginary fairy tale will dissolve between shopping and screams, banking and school lifts, dinners and lack of sleep. If you could only discover this, but understandably, Barry won't hear of it. Maybe I'm the one who is losing my mind. And of course, in reality I could never put the girls through that.

You tell me that you love both of us, in different ways. After considerable thought, I decide that I can try to accept this. I want to keep our family together despite everything. I am open-minded. Maybe society or Western religion has conned us into believing that we should be monogamous when we aren't actually built for it. I make all sorts of excuses. In my heart, I still expect that you will one day see the truth. You don't love her. This is all in your head.

From the time my life changed I started seeing Susie, a therapist. I visit her regularly, once a week, sometimes more. The few psychologists I've seen in my life were dull with no outstanding features. I can't remember them in any detail, what they looked like or even their names. Susie is not a psychologist; she is what you could call a spiritual therapist. Her house is eccentric, full of Eastern carvings and crystals. The space is warm and welcoming. Susie is full of life, vibey and funky. Her cropped gray hair perfectly outlines her high cheekbones and smiling tanned face. She dresses in bright colors and wears strings of over-sized beads around her neck. The first time I met with her, she was nothing like I expected. I relayed my dire story as we sat in her therapy room. Somehow we still managed to laugh and fell into perfectly natural chatter over our coffee and cake. I liked her immediately. At the end of that session, she said, "You know, it seems to me that your main problem is that you haven't learned to love yourself." At the time, I smirked and silently disagreed. Of course I loved myself. My problem was that you didn't love me anymore.

It gives me slight assurance when I read that our star signs are supposedly perfectly matched and that yours and Amanda's are not. I mention this and you snort about not trusting astrology. You have never found a more perfect match than Amanda. All you know is that you are meant to be together. You cling to the similarity between the two of you. You believe that she is your soul mate. That you both live in the same place, and it's not of this world. When you look at her, you see parts of yourself. Mirror images. Reflections of the world through the same eyes.

I am not your mirror and never have been. We are opposites; two different pieces of a puzzle that used to fit seamlessly together. What happened to the pieces?

Staring into the mirror now, the woman I see is unfamiliar. I feel sorry for her. She looks tired. Her cheek bones stand out under the dark circles around her hazel eyes and make her look like a drug addict. Staring closer, I see frown lines dented into her forehead. I have never noticed those before. Then again, I rarely look in the mirror. I think of Amanda – her unblemished cinnamon skin and perfectly smooth face. There is no comparison. Then I remember Susie's words. Susie may be right after all.

By now, you spend much of the day in tears and fall into bed sobbing at night. I continue to hide all this from Jane and Rose and keep up the happy façade. At night once they go to sleep, I continue the cheerful act, lest I fall head first into a sadness I may never find my way out of.

There are days you can't make it to your newspaper job. I have to call your boss to make excuses. I know that what you really need is serious professional help in the form of psychotherapy but when I dare to bring it up again, you refuse assertively. You are one of the most stubborn people I know and you do not, under any circumstance, do doctors in any shape or form. I think back to a time you had double pneumonia and got through it with the help of a doctor friend who also happened to be a musician. He visited you daily under the guise of tea and kept a close eye on you. You were lucky to have made it. I have only managed to get you to a doctor twice in the past eight years. Once for an abscess that needed to be lanced and treated with antibiotics and another time when you had a motorbike accident and needed x-rays.

One night you bring home a comprehensive and amusing list of phobias. There is a name for every single phobia that exists, including ones I not heard of before. We laugh at them. Then you soberly point out that you have every single one on the list. This is called pan-phobia, the fear of everything. I can't find one that describes mine; it isn't on the list. The only one I can think of is the fear of losing you.

10

You've only been home for a month when you decide to leave for a second time. You have a romantic idea of staying at the Blue Waters Hotel on the beachfront for a few months. You have a crazy notion that if you are there, Amanda will come to you. How I will explain to a four and five-year-old that you're leaving again? I decide to tell them that Daddy is going to be staying in a hotel for a while to finish his book.

Any thought I had of you staying home or us working our marriage out, even with a mistress, fades away. My loyal girl friends, who have been doing their best to support me, insist that I give up on you. They protectively call you a bastard, an adulterer, and not worth my time or attention. I ask myself if I am the fool. Am I letting you manipulate and trample all over me as friends complain that I am? I see it more as though you are crushing yourself slowly and without any form of therapy, you are in need of my help. Marriage aside, I care about you and cannot abandon you now.

We somehow find the money to pay a large deposit to secure your hotel room. You take your computer, a few belongings and a bottle of whiskey. Whiskey tea with one sugar is one of your preferred nighttime drinks, particularly when you are writing. There is a plan to continue with the novel you began some time ago but haven't worked on in a while. The story is set in a small farm town, not far from Durban, where you lived when you were a child. You have been back to visit, walk around and take pictures. The girls and I came with you on that trip last year.

Your old farm house was derelict and abandoned. We peered in windows as you showed us your childhood bedroom and the kitchen where you remembered your mother cooking chickens that your father would bring home from work. There was a section of overgrown bamboo that you pointed out, a secret magical place where Ruth and you had created a crystal garden. The girls ran around excitedly and begged you to share more stories. When we were in the barn, you reached up into the rafters and to your surprise, found that the large glass marble you hid as a young boy was still there. You dusted it off and gave it to Rose.

The characters in your novel are taken from people you have met and the lead character is based primarily on yourself. I picture the old-fashioned black and white image in your mind: a writer typing away furiously in the hotel room; stubbing out a cigarette into an overfull ashtray and taking a sip of whiskey tea while considering the next thought. In between, there are secretive visits from your mistress. Afterwards, while she lies and breathes in time to the ocean's lull, you get up out of bed naked and carry on hammering away at the keyboard, pouring out the ideas that race through your mind.

You have been in your hotel room for a week but I haven't seen it yet. We meet on the beach and talk while the girls make elaborate castles in the sand. Your room is on the eighth floor and has a tiny balcony where you can sit and watch the sea across the road. You complain that it's lonely and you still toss and cry at night. Amanda hasn't been to see you and you haven't written a word. You look forlorn. A few days later I receive an e-mail message which makes me feel ill.

From: 'Stuart'
To: 'Robyn'
Sent: 06 April 2006 03:52 PM

I am terribly afraid. Afraid that Amanda will vanish from my life, that I will be left completely at sea – I live on hope and fractions of time and it is wrecking me slowly but I can't do anything about it. I have had my self-control disappear and am at her mercy and must rely on her for my safety and sanity. A perilous place, probably, but, as I said, there is nothing I can do. Helpless.

I am afraid of the look Jane gave me when you left the beach the other night, a sad little face. I am afraid of losing you, whom I love but it is a love eclipsed by another love that I am trapped in – willingly and light, free, when we are together, desperate and filled with tears when we are not. Much of this love has massive physical overtones, something that stretches into a longing that I have yet to explore and discover, enjoy and challenge, somewhere that I have not always felt is approachable with you. I am afraid of having this denied me.

I am afraid that my heart is black, manipulative, conniving and greedy, needy, cruel, vain, selfish, weak and miserable. This makes me burn at night and I cry too much when nobody is watching.

I am afraid of being labeled a whoremonger and an infidel, afraid, despite what reason tells me that others' opinions aren't important, that these opinions run my life and I have not enough personal character to overcome this. I am not a whoremonger or an infidel, and I do want the girls and am shattered by how savage and filthy people are.

I am not perfect, in fact, I am a fuck up – but I am still here on this planet along with everyone else and will not be judged by anybody. Barry is an expert on information and he will do all he can to foul me in Amanda's mind and this makes me afraid and angry.

And I am most afraid that, in two years time, there is a possibility I'll be the saddest fucker on earth with absolutely nothing. No Amanda, no you, no home, no kids, no hope. Then I will die.

11

It has been just over two months since I last saw Amanda at the music festival. I call a meeting with her in a faceless bar. It is my intent to urge her to make a choice – is it Barry or you she wants? She can't have both. I have witnessed two grown men falling apart; crying over a heartache caused by one woman.

Barry and I have been chatting almost every day. Some nights we meet and drink too much wine while discussing our similar predicaments; our fears or possible options. Your take is that Barry is phoning me for information and you warned me to be careful. We probably both want to get information from each other. I have tried to find out what Amanda is thinking but he doesn't seem to know.

Now it's time for me to speak to her. I can't stand by and watch you being so miserable. Amanda arrives after I do and looks nervous, but cool and compelling at the same time. She sits down and then in a sugary voice asks, "Are you here to tell me what a naughty girl I've been?"

I should slap her, but I am softer than I expect to be. Amanda has that way with people. She comes across as self-assured, but possesses a fundamental tenderness and vulnerability that suggests she needs to be handled with care.

I begin by making it clear that you are falling apart and that she needs to either follow through and come to you or end it now. She tries to explain that she is between a rock and a hard place. What rock? Which hard place? I calmly endeavor to impress on her that it is simply a decision. When I mention that the reason I am doing all of this is out of deep concern and love for you, she asks me, of all things, why you and I don't just try and work things out! What is she playing at? Of course I bloody well want to work things out. Why the hell does she think I'm here?

Before I can give her an answer, my cell phone vibrates and I pick it up. A friend's voice apologizes for having to call and as he goes on speaking, the room goes dark and the red of my wine turns to blood. Daniel is dead. I stand up and start pacing as I listen to the details of how he hung himself. How his wife, Carrie, with their baby in her arms, found him hanging in their garden earlier today. Daniel was a friend of yours. Carrie is in my book club.

Amanda stares at my stunned face as I take a huge gulp of wine. Shaking fiercely, I am even more determined to finish my talk with her. To say what I came to say. To make sure that I will never find myself in the harrowing situation that Carrie is in tonight. Amanda seems to be stuck in performer mode and I cannot determine if anything she says or does is genuine. She is sweet as honey and appears to want the best for all of us. I express that I am trying my best, but that at the moment it seems pointless, as you only want her. You are waiting for her at the Blue Waters Hotel. She must either come to you or allow you to move on; let you know that there is no hope. All I see are her huge green eyes, wary and cautious. We talk for hours, circling around her rock and her hard place with no resolution. She doesn't seem to understand the risk she is taking in not making a decision; that this isn't a game. I am unable to concentrate; my thoughts are unhinged by what has happened with Daniel and what I fear could happen to you. I have to leave her and come to you.

It's late by the time I get to your hotel and come up to your room for the first time. You are eager to hear what Amanda had to say but disappointed when I describe her as vague and evasive, not knowing what to do. We sit on your tiny hotel balcony, listening to the ocean as I update you about Daniel. I lose my grip, and all of my dread and horror comes out in a torrent of tears. As my sobs come harder and harder, I take in jagged gasps of air, feeling as though I am suffocating. All the while you sit perfectly still, without moving a muscle. I cannot bring myself to voice the real reason I am in this state. I am unable to speak of the relentlessly terrifying reality with which my days are filled. The truth I live with every day is that the phone call earlier could have been about you. And tonight, I could have so easily been Carrie.

12

It's still dark in our bedroom and the strong metallic smell of blood fills the air. You popped in to visit the girls on your way to work. Our white cat is in a box I set up for her on the floor near the bed. From our bird's eye view, we all watch in wonder as she delivers one lone kitten. Lying on the bed together, Jane and Rose gaze as the mother cat tenderly cleans her new baby and I sneak a glance at you, trying to decipher the look on your face. I am vaguely aware of the presence of life and death and that thin line that runs between them.

Jane and Rose stay with the kitten and we head to the veranda for a morning coffee. The sunlight ruptures through the trees and explodes around us. I feel exhilarated from the birth but am pulled between that buzz and your gloom. The darkness in your soul. The unbearable heaviness of your heart. You look beaten and helpless.

Silence. You have zilch to say. We've discussed everything so many times. I have nothing to talk about either. I can't ask you how the hotel is, how work is, how you are… I know the answers to all those questions. So I sip my coffee in the odd space between us. Looking at the birds in the garden, I think of flying off with them. Somewhere happier or lighter. Free. I swallow away my helplessness with another sip of coffee and then notice that it's you who's crying again. Without saying a word, I wipe a tear from your face with my thumb and kiss your cheek before turning to go inside and check on the girls. Jane has decided to call the new white kitten, Cloud, saying that it reminds her of one.

I can't blame your depression on the anesthetic from your vasectomy earlier this week. You are terrified of hospitals. I had suggested the operation mostly since I didn't want the girls to have a complicated half sibling. I waited for you even though you implored me to leave. The sterile white environment gave me a chill. I felt sorry for you lying pale and vulnerable in a place you despised. Hospitals, you said, are the epitome of weakness and vile humanity, a grim reminder of our mortality. When your eyes flickered open, there was a moment of recognition before you glared at me and barked, "GO AWAY."

I turned and headed outside for a cigarette and a tearful phone call to Ruth. I should have left. Let you find your own way back to the hotel. But of course, I stayed. Five minutes later I got an urgent text message to get you out of there. I waited for you at the car. Back at your hotel, I realized the drip was still in your arm; you had left without checking out. You were soft again and apologized for shouting at me, explaining that when you woke up in the hospital you longed to see her. But I am the one who always shows up. With your experience as a medic in the army, you were able to remove the drip from your own arm. I waited while you took a shower and we inspected your tiny wound. Then I kissed you lightly before leaving you on the bed in tears. She had promised to visit you soon.

I am worn out when I climb into bed tonight. The girls lie as close as they can to Cloud's box. As I drift off to sleep I see red behind my eyelids and believe I can still smell blood. I will clean up tomorrow. The sleepy thought crosses my mind that I will never again experience a birth of my own. Only death. That part of the cycle I can't escape.

13

I hate shopping. Shopping centers are to be avoided at all costs. There are too many people and I feel like a stranger. These days, grocery shopping makes me teary. Everywhere are memories of you. I've taken to doing my shopping online to escape this task. But on days like today, I need bread and milk and something to feed the girls for dinner. Another effort. In the vegetable aisle, I subconsciously head towards the beetroot. Piled up on the cart, they are round and plump and the color of deep red wine. You love beetroot. You deem them to be the cleansers of our bodies and souls. One of the few pure things left in life. You love them best when they are boiled; crunchy and salted or sliced into thick wedges and preserved in vinegar. Every few months you go through weeks of beetroot cravings, when searching for goodness. I feel the rock hard bulbs and pack two bunches into my basket. You need beetroots now. Simple things that you love will surely bring you back; back to the days of good cooking and wholesomeness. I can make them for you the way you enjoy them. If you visit, I will feed you beetroot. And later, you can laugh at the way your wee turns red; showing the girls like you used to do. It would be good to see you laugh. I forget what else I came to get, and leave without the milk. Again.

On the drive home I think of how I have never paid attention to beetroot before. Jane hates vegetables, but Rose has developed your fondness for them along with many other things. It's remarkable how similar the two of you are. Jane reminds me more of myself; quick and alert, sensible and reliable.

I carry the small bag of groceries inside, set it down on the counter and put a pot of water on to boil. Looking at your belongings around the house – old photos, artworks and books – I wonder if I ever actually listened to you. You spoke of their history but I don't remember the details. In the beginning, those things seemed unimportant. Of course, I listened to you. But the important thing was how much you loved me, how that made me feel. Is that why I feel so dreadful now? Your belongings are in the house, but you are not here. I am alone. I slice the beetroot and stare at the wedges trying to see their purity. I feel nothing. I'll make them for Rose because you aren't coming home. When they are cooked I put them onto newspaper as you used to do and sprinkle them with salt. I bite into one. They aren't that bad. But one piece is all I can stomach. I have no appetite. I've hardly eaten in months. Food is such an irrelevant part of my days. I set some aside for Rose and put the rest into a jar of vinegar. I'll keep them for you, a gift for your next visit.

The girls and I walk down the road to pick some flowers from a neighbor's hedge. I arrange them in a jug on the kitchen table in an attempt to create beauty in the obviously empty house. I tidy up so that everything is perfect and I'm the perfect housewife, just in case you come home. I light my favorite incense and have a long bath with lavender to calm down, but I don't feel peaceful. In bed, I read the girls a story and then we cuddle up together.

"Mommy, when is Daddy coming home?" Rose asks.

I sigh, "Daddy will come home soon, I'm sure."

"But why does he have to sleep at work?" Her wide eyes question me sincerely and I am almost tempted to tell them the truth, tell them everything and then I remember that they are only four and five years old and that it isn't fair. I want to make life beautiful and safe and loving for them.

"Because that is what he has decided to do right now."

"But why?" she whines.

Jane pipes up, "Rose, Dad has to because he is writing a book."

"Oh," says Rose, as if that explains it all.

"Time to get some sleep girls," I say and kiss their foreheads.

"Mamma, can you sing?" says Jane. And I sing them our lullaby until they fall sound asleep.

I call you at the hotel. You sound terrible. You can hardly speak. The phone call is short and uncomfortable and afterwards I wish there was more I could do. I can't sleep and I spend the night looking at the garden through the smoke of my hundredth cigarette.

I'm exhausted. I don't suppose you have even the slightest idea of the hell I have been through in the past few months, or if you are even able to care. All you worry about now is if she is coming to you or not. I already know the answer to that. She won't come. I wish you were safe at home and none of this had happened. I want to go back to the days when you loved me, back to the days when we were still your everything. Your two little girls and me.

14

The click of the front door being unlocked wakes me up. In the early dawn light, I watch you slip into bed and curl up against Rose. Your face is wet with tears; your eyes signal panic. You whisper, "I'm not going to make it. Can I come home?"

Nodding, I check to make sure the girls haven't woken up before creeping out of bed and heading straight for the kettle. I could do with a strong coffee. There's time to speak before the girls will be up. Sitting outside, you say, "I am dying alone in that hotel room. The pull of the sea is too strong."

You barely lasted three weeks there. Amanda came to see you a couple of times in the bar for a drink, and the one time she came up to your room, you assure me, nothing happened. She arrived last night to say that she had decided to put all her energies into making it work with Barry. It seemed she was trying to say goodbye or that was your understanding. After she left, you went for a long walk along the beach and threw your cell phone into the sea. The phone had been driving you crazy. It was your connection and communication to Amanda. Every waking minute was spent with it by your side, in case it beeped the message you had been waiting for; the one to announce that she was coming. Now you are devastated and ask if you can stay home for good this time.

"Sure. The girls will be happy about that." I nod as I do a quick check to make sure that they are still safe in bed. I must think of them. You and I can live together as friends and see how it pans out. At least if you are home, I can keep a close eye on you. I can't help but wonder if my recent meeting with Amanda had anything to do with her decision.

We lose the deposit on the hotel room, but it doesn't matter. Money has become one of those unimportant things. I help you move. You can scarcely cope with niceties and insignificant practical measures of any sort. So I check you out of the hotel, trying to be polite to the condescending man behind the reception desk. I concentrate on the ridiculous glasses slipping down his nose as he takes his time doing the necessary paperwork. He is falsely engaging and I have to control the urge to grab his neck tie, yank him towards me and say, "Listen here little man, move it along, I haven't got all day."

He cannot be expected to know what I am going through. As we carry your computer to the car, I think about all your romantic notions of writing a novel in a hotel room for six months like some undiscovered author. Smoking cigarettes and drinking whiskey in between visits from Amanda. I feel sorry for you. I feel sorry for me.

Every day I have to wonder how dire your emotions will be, and deal with the effects of this on me and on the girls. We return to our nightly ritual of sitting on the veranda, drinking. There is a lot of silent time but some nights we discuss our childhoods or share stories that we've never told before. For the most part, you still speak about Amanda. Everything you say concerning the two of you, I've heard before. Where you started out by saying that you think you might be able to find a safe place to put your feelings for her and carry on with your life, you now fear that this is no longer possible. You cannot accept that there is no chance or future for the two of you.

"Come on," I contest, "She's married. She has never left him before and she never will. You are not her first and you won't be the last. She is not coming!"

I try to convince you that even if she did love you she would have changed her mind about being with you now that you are behaving like a possessive, manipulative, and emotional mad man. I beg you once again to get help; to consider that your emotional condition may be treatable with medication, but you still won't hear of it.

I fear that this will destroy first you and then me. I get frustrated watching you spiraling downwards towards disaster. I sit by, helpless to show you the truth or help you move on. You proclaim you love me too, but I don't see it. I don't see anything but misery and ruin. Our love is not enough for you, I cannot understand this. You have a life. Right here in front of you. A life with me and your girls. The practical side of me does not understand your inability to make a choice.

I think of how we used to joke about our few differences. Things like you preferring to sleep with the windows open whereas I wanted them closed, or you being a morning person while I was not. They were such small differences and we never fought over them. This is the first time we don't agree on something so important. I insist that this is merely a choice; encouraging you to be heartbroken, bawl, howl, and then choose to move on. You state without a doubt that this is not a choice for you. You have no choice in this matter. We have been round in circles; how many more times will I have to hear the same stuff? Sitting on the veranda, every night, feels like *déjà vu*.

One night you criticize my monotone voice. You mean the voice I use when I am struggling to stay composed, and barely managing to get the words out. Amanda, of course, does not have a monotone voice. What is it that appeals to you in her that I am lacking? Did I lose myself in motherhood? Did I become boring and responsible? Possibly it's that I don't sing like an angel, dance in the rain, read the same books you do or look as if

I've just stepped out of a magazine. But I can hold a house together when it should be falling apart.

I've heard of marriages that have lasted through rough times. If Amanda meant what she said about working her marriage out with Barry, maybe there is still hope for us. The same glimmer of hope that teases me in some of your confusing messages.

From: 'Stuart'
To: 'Robyn'
Sent: 09 June 2006 11:13 AM

A long day ahead and woke up bewildered and blue, angry and sad. More and more I am convinced that life is short and we should be living it to the full, without restrictions or fear, both of which rule all our lives. I wonder how much longer I can go on being sad. But you must know how I value your presence and love, we will be alright. Silence is stronger than a million gushed truths and I am prone to gushing and wish I had more layers to cover what is so close to the surface – more mute and stifle. Amanda's silence is killing but admirable in strength, which just makes me madder.

Your balance of speech and reflection seems whole and I try to take this as an example, which works when I'm with you but crumbles when alone or sometimes at night. I don't want to lose you – besides the girls, you are the only valuable thing in my life. Thank you for being with me – I love you.

15

When our small white kitten, Cloud, is eight weeks old, I discover she is deaf. It's not something I am seeking out. But one day, it dawns on me that she doesn't come when I call her or wake up with noise. I experiment by clapping loudly in her ear while she is sleeping but there is no response. After several more tests, I miserably conclude that she can hear nothing at all. Jane is sad about this too and takes care of her with tireless devotion. In order for us to make out where she is at all times, I adorn her with a petite blue collar and bell.

She is not the only deaf one. You are in your own world and seem to notice less and less around you. Your heart is sad and distant, in another place, another dream that will not happen. This is a reality which you cannot accept. Your denial keeps you caged in the very place that you so desperately struggle to escape. You long for a life you will never have, and find no happiness in anything else. The girls, whose names you have tattooed on your arm, keep you safe, you allege. But even they are not sufficient consolation for the void you feel.

All the inspirations I have been reading about up until this point hover in my mind, but I don't seem to be able to apply any of it. Even though I have learned how to meditate and understand the value of living in the present moment, nothing has prepared me for this present moment. I don't want to be here. I want to be in the past when you loved me or in the future when everything is sorted out. There are words and thoughts in my head all day and night. They circle around like eagles looking for their prey. Will my marriage last? Will I stay in this beautiful house? Will the girls be okay? Will you make it through this? I long for you to take control of your feelings. Accept that you have a wonderful house, a beautiful family who loves you, a job that you enjoy, and you have your music.

I focus on talking you through the depths of despair to try and get you to a point of seeing some light. No matter what positive or constructive guidance I have to offer, it lands on deaf ears. I wish I could give you a magical pill to make you realize all the good in your life and move away from the horrible place of gloom. Instead, I try to think of a way to give you the anti-depressants you refuse. Maybe I can slip them to you each day. I visit my doctor under the pretense that I am depressed. Who wouldn't be in my circumstances? Using the anti-depressants he prescribes for me, I do countless trials to find a way to secretly get you to take them. Crushing them up as finely as possible in the mortar and pestle, I mix them into a whiskey tea, with lots of sugar. No matter how well I crush them – and I become an expert – white grains sink to the bottom, and the last sip is bitter. I daren't ever attempt this experiment on you. You will be furious if you catch me.

You continue to wallow in your sorrow, ignoring anything else with a tunnel vision of that one unobtainable beauty that exists in your imagination, a solitary place where you have chosen to live. You maintain you are not meant for this world and I understand. You are different. That's one of the things I love about you. It should be a gift, not a curse.

My dear Nana died in her home in October 2005. I stayed with her from the previous night when she went into a coma. In the morning, I sat with her and whispered in her ear, "Let go Nana. You can go and be with Grandpa now."

Then I hummed to her; the French song she used to sing to me as a child. Shortly afterwards, she took two deep breaths and then lay motionless. I watched her body for a while, aware that she was no longer there.

It took me three days to clear out her home and go through the memories; the possessions that we gather in this world. Along with a few other items, I brought home all of her medicine. I hid the morphine tablets from the girls in our old-fashioned electricity box, too high to reach. Then I forgot about them.

How you discovered them during this dark time, I'll never know. You couldn't read the label; it was too worn and so you had no clue what they were. You swallowed four. When I asked you what on earth you were thinking, you said, "Well, I knew they must be something strong or they wouldn't be hidden." I shake my head at your audacity. The next day when you are out, I flush the remaining tablets down the toilet. There are too many to leave lying around with you as you are.

I monitor you more carefully than ever. I can no longer judge what you may be capable of doing. You seem to have crossed a line; a boundary that was there for you all along but that you had previously managed to steer clear of. You have always been more daring than most. Doing everything larger and more extreme than anyone else I've met. This quality can be good, or at least I used to think of it in that light. Now I'm not so sure. I'm not certain of much these days. I am careful now; careful of what I say and how I say it, of so many things. I have to smooth everything over to protect the girls' happiness; to make sure they don't notice that life is so different now. I feel like a cheerleader in a fancy uniform, with a plastic smile and a broken heart.

16

The ramshackle wood and iron house next door is up for sale. It has an overgrown sprawling garden that cuts into ours with an L shape. Since having the girls we have dreamt of buying it to extend our property. An enormous pear tree at the back is perfect for a tree house. There is no for-sale sign out front, but the elderly man has passed away and the widow has agreed to give us first option to purchase. This seems like the ideal timing. If our marriage doesn't work out, you could live in the adjacent house and the girls could scamper between the two. On the other hand, we could rent out the house and still use part of the garden.

I leap into action by phoning the bank to apply for an additional mortgage, which is approved right away. Our nightly conversations change. Interest stirs up in you as we begin designing the tree house and contemplating a swimming pool. A creative project is just what you need. We throw around ideas of you living next door and building a veranda. Planning a future, however uncertain, could provide a reason for you to stick around. The widow moves out and I wait in anticipation for her to return my phone calls so that we can finalize the sale. The girls sneak through the fence to explore the garden, already claiming it as their own.

On a bitter and windy night, a few weeks later, you arrive home from a jaunt to the harbor. Your sandy hair is frenzied as you take off your bike helmet. Holding a quart of beer and flinging yourself into the rocking chair, you raise your chin in a serious manner. There is an air of resoluteness in your square shoulders which gives me the idea that you have something significant to say. A determined groove sets in your forehead when you break the silence with one sentence, "I've made a decision."

Just that. In the space following that sentence, I consider what this could mean. After a time of no choice you've made a decision. Could it be for me and the girls? You take a slow sip from the large green beer bottle and narrow your eyes before continuing, "I don't want to be here anymore."

What? I think. You're leaving? Have you chosen her? As you carry on speaking with a chilling calm, I realize that this is far worse than you leaving home.

"I can no longer be a part of this world."

Your flat announcement expands to fill all the empty space. It is an avalanche threatening to crush me. You have decided to die.

Up until this point, your threats, although frightening, have been vague. Now you are devastatingly clear. For the second time, I grab my keys and cigarettes and walk up the stairs; away from things I can't listen to anymore. Once I am in the car, I realize the only friends who'll be awake at this hour are Beverley and her husband David. Your friend Beverley with whom you shared your first mountain threat. I head straight there. David immediately offers me tequila, listening patiently as my questions tumble out. When are you planning this? How long do we have? Which day will you not come home? When will be the last morning I kiss you goodbye; the last time the girls see you? David pours me more tequila; there's not much else he can do.

While driving home I feel calmer. It might be the tequila. But something else has changed; I surrender. I realize that I cannot save you, though I will not stop trying. There is no one that can save you outside of yourself. I manage to sleep and morning brings with it another light. I tell you that I know there is nothing I can do to change your mind. I am not responsible for your decision. You do a turn around, promising that you didn't mean it. You verify that you are not leaving and beg me not to tell anyone.

In the coming days, I notice a transformation; a change for the better. I read a message that you send to Caron, a friend of yours in Canada, which confirms my optimism. But with your unpredictable mood swings, I have no idea how seriously to take you.

From: 'Stuart'
To: 'Caron'
Sent: 27 July 2006 10:57 PM

Hello. The girls are asleep, Robyn is working tonight setting up a clothes market she and a friend do and the house is really quiet. I have a glass of wine and will think of cuddling up to the little monkeys shortly in welcome rest.

My heart is a lot more peaceful than it has been for ages – I had a drastic night on Tuesday when all resistance crumbled and succumbing to the ocean's pull was inevitable, just a matter of time. The world of men and women can be a terrifying place sometimes, what they are capable of, what I am capable of. But then, between blessed Robyn and, perhaps my guardian angel – who I think has been measuring me and my worth – I surfaced and will make every effort not to return to that hopeless and hellish place, although I know it will always be there. Soul management is needed and I realize that I rely on and need help with this from those that I care about – Robyn, Amanda, the girls, Ruth, a few friends. This is contrary to your maxims that we are born alone, must manage alone and will die alone and must look after ourselves because no one else will. True words, but I am not that strong and must build into the picture a reliance on those who don't inhabit the fridge-world and may understand my complicated heart.

Robyn is an extraordinary and sovereign creature who I know loves me and I, in turn, her, because she loves me unconditionally as well as because of who she is; my best friend, the mother of our children, the most open-minded and understanding woman that has so much to teach and give. Amanda is my muse and soul mate and, despite situational stuff and doubts, loves me as I do her and our distances will survive because of this. Robyn and Amanda understand that love is not always something given to one person alone to keep tethered and guarded, it comes in many non-standard colors, non-Western, and both are big enough to endorse it and knowing this has taken a weight from me – that of guilt and the green spiders of disappointing someone. Both of them are recipients of my desires, but as this is, for me, more of a head thing, I will negotiate this as it surfaces – with Robyn, because the damage of this with Amanda – through Barry – is unbearable to negotiate and I can't afford any more tears. I am just feeling grateful for blessings I have instead of tangling myself up in losses and fears, which come to me too easily. Is this the dawn of happiness again, or a moment's delusion? Wily time will tell, but the moment is good.

In all this is you, too, dearest – the million miles away ear that I bend and stumble towards with questions and answers. Love Stuart

17

Winter is disappearing. The moon is waning and you are vanishing along with it. It didn't last; the brief illusion of hope that emerged for three short weeks. The appearance of your former self that told me you never wanted to feel the way you had been feeling ever again. At first I watched skeptically as you jumped up in the morning, made breakfast for the girls; chatting and even smiling. You began bringing me coffee in bed like you used to and kissed me goodbye before leaving for work. At the end of the day, you'd arrive home with news and eagerly help with cooking dinner and cleaning up. At night, you'd scoop me up in your arms, telling me how you much you loved me. And for that short while, I felt that perhaps everything really could be okay. It seemed that it was still possible to step over the last seven months towards an amended horizon. But soon it was all gone again.

There was nothing to celebrate today, on our eighth wedding anniversary. As I drove home, I saw a SOLD sign on the house next door. Sold? To whom? The elderly widow promised us first option. We offered her the price she wanted. This was going to be our house. Your house. I call the estate agent who tells me that the widow had never mentioned us and the house was now sold. I break down. The girls will not have their big garden with a tree house. You will never be able to build that veranda. No teas and guitar playing next door. We could've still been a family living in two houses. The girls would still have their dad. I believed that love could be split across two houses or even across two women. The sold sign confirms to me that it can't be.

I think back to a story you told me of a time you were nine years old and spent every afternoon after school lovingly building a double-storey dollhouse out of cardboard for your sister Ruth. You put so much effort into each detail and when you gave it to her she played with it for three weeks, and then it lay demolished and flattened, discarded; a thing that belonged to neither of you.

Curled up on the couch together a week after our anniversary, we listen to the same Rod Stewart CD all evening on repeat. Neither of us has the energy to get up and change it. I feel that I am at a crossroads and I have to talk to you. I need to know that there is still a chance for us, that we will make it. With just these words, I can carry on. I can keep on believing. But you aren't listening; instead you are talking about yourself. I become quiet, searching for any last glimmer of hope in your words. Then you say you have something to tell me. I listen in anticipation and fear. As the story unfolds, any hope I have dwindles and evaporates into nothing. A few nights ago, you'd met Amanda down at the docks. Your usual meeting spot, near the two herons that live in the bay. You hadn't mentioned this to me at the time as you usually did. So I listen carefully and I hear that Amanda cupped your face in her hands and looked you straight in the eyes as she said, "I love you Stuart."And then you kissed; a long and gentle kiss. You are crying while you tell me this, telling me how much you love each other. How tragic it is that you aren't together. As you cry, I hold you. Rod Stewart is still playing. I hold you for a long while, and in my heart I know. I know there is only one thing to do.

18

All of the next day I feel ill and undecided. But by the time you come home from work, I am strangely resolute. I know that I can't do this anymore, we can't. We sit down to tea on the veranda. The girls are watching a movie. There is no easy way to say it, so I just start. I tell you how much I love you and that although I still understand that it's possible for you to love two people, I can't live like this anymore. Crying so much that I can barely speak, I make it clear that I can't go on watching you being so unhappy without being willing to do anything about it. I can't live with your suffering without any thought for myself and I can't put the girls through this for another day. I just can't do any of it anymore.

You sit dead still and quiet in your rocking chair. I am aware that my words are killing you but I keep going. Saying that one of us needs to make a decision and seeing as you can't, I will do it. I will make a decision for all of us. I have to be strong. Inside I am breaking as I assert that my decision is final, even though my heart is screaming NO! I ask you to move out. I will help you find a proper place. We must make this as easy as possible in the situation. You say nothing and go and lie down with the girls in front of their movie.

I have to get out of the house. I meet Lisa for a drink. She is supportive and proud of me. I know deep down that I have made the best decision. I have no idea how I will manage to stick to it, but I will try. When I come home, you are asleep, wrapped around the girls. I stare at the three of you, I feel like I am ripping you apart. I am not sure if I can stick to this.

You don't utter a word for the next two days. My decision is anything but final. I secretly long for you to be shocked into your senses and realize that you can't lose us. You can't lose everything over an imaginary relationship, something that will never materialize. In an e-mail message to you, I explain that this isn't what I want but that seeing as it has come to this, we should try and be gentle about it, especially for the girls. We'll be friends forever, I tell you. I will always love you; I want to make sure you understand that. You don't speak a word but you send me a message two days later.

From: 'Stuart'
To: 'Robyn'
Sent: 06 October 2006 09:33 AM

Sorry I can't talk – don't know what to say, if there is anything. I'll go to Cape Town but will need to find some money and make some plans. I can't stay in the same town as the two people I love but can't be with. I need to stay in the same country as the girls and be able to see them from time to time. I can't think of this yet, it is too sad.

I don't know how long I will be in Cape Town, but if I can get a job and place to stay and don't go mad, I will stay indefinitely. Let's not get legally divorced because it will compromise practical benefits. I will be gentle and fair but am also going to try to be decisive, helped by your decision, which is a good thing because I am useless at being decisive. I don't want to have to say goodbye to the girls. I don't want to speak to anyone.

Tonight after you have gone to sleep with the girls, I sit on the veranda alone. There is a long slow solid rain that is not common during October. It is as if Mother Nature is pouring out the tears that I long to cry. I take a pen and paper and write you a letter, one I never give you.

6 October 2006

My dearest Stuart

You're still here, it's Friday night and you've gone to bed. I can't talk to you now either because if I start, both our tears and hurt will be more than we can bear. We've got this far and we mustn't turn back, I know that. Neither of us have the strength to do this, but we must somehow find the strength. If I let my tears start, I feel like they will never end. So I will post this letter to Ruth in Cape Town and it may get there after you arrive. I don't know what to say or where to start but we both know it all anyway. I just want to come and get you out of bed and beg and plead with you not to go, but that would not help either of us. I need to find the strength somewhere inside to be strong for all of us. Maybe after you've gone, I can let it all out and cry all the tears that have been coming for all this time. You will always be everywhere with me, in my thoughts and heart. Be strong, dear friend, our paths will meet again. I hope you find what you are looking for. I know I live in reality but sometimes I wish there were a place for all my dreams. Make the best of it, Stuart.

love Robyn

Through an e-mail message I find out that you managed to negotiate a job transfer to Cape Town, same hours, same salary.

As soon as the rain stops, you say you will leave and drive all the way down on your motorbike and stay with Ruth.

I sit Jane and Rose down and say, "I have some very sad news. Daddy is moving to Cape Town to live with Ruth and work there."

Rose wants to know who will cuddle her at night; Jane asks a lot of questions. I explain that sometimes Mommies and Daddies live in different houses because they love each other as friends. The girls are both dreadfully miserable and follow you around like lost puppies.

On Sunday night, you and I speak for the first time since I asked you to leave. You have been drinking and say that you don't really care; you aren't in love with me anyway but that the worst thing in the whole world is leaving the girls.

The next day, I decide to go through your bottom drawer before you leave and take everything with you. The drawer is filled with all your personal papers including letters and I have never invaded your privacy before. I feel terrible even now, but I am sure that once you've gone I will never know the truth. A last chance to try and find some proof that Amanda's feelings are as you tell me they are. A final opportunity to figure out if you are completely deluded or if you have been telling me the truth all along. I sit guiltily and shuffle through papers I recognize, song compositions and poems.

Then I find them, an envelope of letters. I shudder and slip them out. I read them slowly. It is all as you have told me. Amanda has been declaring her love and the letters are wordy and seductive. They date back to six months before I heard the words. There aren't many here but you have told me before that there have been reams and reams. You carry them around with you in your backpack everywhere you go. With the confirmation I was searching for, I sigh and put them back as I found them.

It takes four days for the rain to stop. You wake me up early to let me know that you are leaving. Jane helps you pack. Rose watches a movie. When you are ready to leave, you sit down next to Rose to say goodbye. She asks you where you are going and when you answer Cape Town, even though we've told her several times, her face crumples into tears. Jane follows you while you pack your motorbike.

You hand both the girls a letter and ask me to read it to them every day. It reads – 'I love you more than the sun, the moon, the stars and the sea. Love Daddy.'

Just before you drive off, you squeeze my shoulder and your parting words to me are, "If you see Amanda, please tell her I am always there for her."

PART III

19

The house is quiet and empty the moment you ride off. It is a different type of silence. You haven't just gone for a drink or a drive. You haven't popped out to the supermarket to fetch us milk. You aren't going to the post office to collect a parcel for me. You have gone. And this time, you aren't coming back; not ever. I know this because I know you. I listen to your motorbike for as long as I can hear it. Then I think I can still hear it. Maybe if I race down the road after you, I can find you and beg you to come home. Explain to you one more time how much I love you, how much we want you to be part of our family. Maybe. If I could just say one word. Stay.

In the stillness, I picture you riding in one direction. Away from us. Then I imagine you turning around and driving home like the wind, realizing you can never go; you can never leave us. But this doesn't happen. Still, for days I listen. I envision you on that old BMW motorbike, the dusty roads imprinting the tear stains down your cheeks. I know through everything you can't bear to leave the girls. If I forget my pain for a second to think of yours, yours is undoubtedly worse. I think of you alone, in horrible modest hotel rooms in the middle of the night, tossing and battling. Sand-crusted hair and cigarette-stained fingers with a worn and tired body that aches far less than your heart. I want to fix you. More than anything, I want to make it better. But I don't know where you are, or how to make anything better anymore.

The girls look pitiful and in order to try and make everything okay I take them to a friend's cottage in the mountains for a few days. My feelings of abandonment and deep sadness are over-ridden with the primary uncertainty of your safety and sanity and with the girls' well being. I want to keep it together for them and make their lives as happy as I can in spite of the dreadful circumstances. If I think too hard about my own feelings now, I may dissolve into a sadness that is bigger than I could cope with, so I keep them safely inside. Part of me thinks that you have no intention of making it to Cape Town, and because of this, the wait seems endless.

Five days after you drive away, my cell phone rings and I recognize Ruth's number. The air is chilly under the clear mountain night sky scattered with stars. Both girls are snug inside next to the fireplace. Your voice is small and distant as you tell me that you have arrived safely in Cape Town. The phone call doesn't make me feel much better; you don't sound well. I speak to Ruth and she confirms that you barely made it. On Saturday late afternoon as you approached Cape Town, even your motorbike gave up. Ruth and Bradley came to your rescue. Ruth adds that when they arrived she hardly recognized you; you looked haggard, worn, and homeless.

20

Your first letter lies opened next to my bed. I almost knock over the half empty cup of coffee as I lean across to reach for it. I hold it against my chest for a while before unfolding it again carefully. Steady breathing assures me that the girls are still fast asleep. I absentmindedly take a sip of the left-over cold coffee from last night before looking down to search the familiar scrawl for more than I found yesterday when I read it for the first time. The tears blur my vision before I even begin.

14 October 2006

My dearest Robyn

I had a whole letter book that I'd written to you, but have thrown it away along with one to Amanda; they are just severe and depressing. I want, with all my heart, for you to be happy, find the love you deserve, be loved for you, and may it flow to our precious little girls, who I can't think of without bursting into tears, as I do now. I don't know how I will survive without them near. What I need to say is: I love you, you are every good thing you know yourself to be and I ask, with all my heart to be forgiven for who I am, what I have done, what I will still do. My love for Amanda is pure, our timing is not. She is my last love and all other loves will be measured against this…

I fear for my life; the pointless beauty that surrounds me is killing me, I am drifting steadily towards madness and alienation; perhaps becoming myself. But for the sake of those who love me – you, Amanda, the girls, my friends and family, I will try as hard as I can to operate and function normally; there are words you have said to me, words Amanda has said to me, the tattoo on my arm (Rosie Jane) that I turn to when I think I can't go on. I must never lose sight of this and ask, plead that you keep sending me words of advice and care; these will be a lifeline for me. I will never leave you or the girls in the lurch – I don't know how I will manage reality, but all my efforts will be for you and the girls. My mind is a fuckup but my heart isn't. I am very afraid of what will become of me. I am not afraid of what will become of you – your beautiful soul will attract the same and you will embrace this as you grow. It will gladden and please my heart knowing you can move inside yourself without fear and live on joy instead, that which is basically your due and which belongs to you. I will think of you always with tenderness and care and you are always free to speak, write, e-mail me, whenever, wherever. I am always glad to hear your voice, see your words. We must live for the day and not look forward to an old age veranda: if we do, we have to remember to act now: we must not say to whomever we are with "phew, we made it," we have to say "phew, it was good." Do not forget this and act now. But be practical – reality is harsh and has no sympathy. Look after the girls with everything you have, wash hair, clip nails, be kind. And tell them every day I love them and am not gone from them; I have them literally under my skin.

My suicidal hours are from midnight to noon – the afternoons and the evenings are manageable. Think of me during that time and know that I am alright. During the other hours, pray to the stars and the sun to guide me, as I do. I will post this letter now, and kiss your forehead.

Love Stuart

Yesterday when Rose stepped on the white Frangipani flowers outside Lisa's house, she stopped and cried so hard that I couldn't understand what she was trying to say. I put down my handbag and keys and crouched next to her as she wept and squeaked.

"What is it my little love?" I asked.

"I shouldn't have told him… Daddy put one of these flowers behind my ear. I told him he mustn't because they are poisoned. But I shouldn't have said that because I love it when my Daddy puts flowers behind my ear, see?"

I tried to calm her down, but she bawled the whole way home in the car. She cried at home when I emptied the post box and hid your first letter in my handbag. In bed, she remembered the white flowers again, and cried herself to sleep. I cried too. I cried for her, for Jane, for me. I sobbed when I read your letter. Then I took a pen and forced myself to write.

20 October 2006

My Dearest Stuart

Thank you for your beautiful letter. I am so happy to know that you and I will be lifelong friends. I love you, you know that. I am glad to have met you and for all the things we have shared, and the many wonderful things you have taught me about myself. And of course, the girls! This, we will always share. The girls, despite the sad stories, will be fine; we will both make sure of this.

I will try, instead of seeing this as an ending, to see it as a new beginning, a new time in our lives, a special friendship, one I hope we will always have. And too, instead of looking at the garden, as I have done, and seeing sadness in the memories of all the plants you planted, I will look after those plants and try to see them as a happy reminder of all you have given me and the girls. Instead of weeping on the veranda, looking at your empty rocking chair, I will try and think happy thoughts of you when I look at it, and send you love. Instead of thinking that I will never again have the chance to touch you, staring into your eyes in the darkness of our room, I will try to remember our love as the gentle love that it was and be happy for the time I had with you. I will try to have no regrets in this life and find freedom in that. I will also allow myself and the girls to be sad if we feel sad. Life is long and we will still have many things to share, just different things. I will not deny my love for you, but will allow that love to find its place in my heart, a place with less hurt. I love you Stuart. My greatest hope for you is that you will one day love yourself too.

love Robyn

21

My therapist Susie has become a lifeline; a common thread woven intimately between the people and weeks of my story, making up a quilt of the whole tale. When you were still at home, I would share every Susie session with you. Even though you chuckled about the new-agedness of it all, you encouraged me to press forward with my therapy. You called Susie my guru. I consider her my support. She helps me untangle the pieces of my day-to-day reality by talking them through and teaching me that the only person I can change is me.

Now that you are gone, Susie has become a salvation for the girls. She was extremely surprised to hear that, between our sessions, I had asked you to leave home and that you had already moved to Cape Town. Jane is older and wiser and gets deeply distressed about everything. You left home a week after her sixth birthday. Not only has she lost her dad, but over the past months, she has had to deal with the loss of her best friend too, Amanda's son. I have run out of excuses as to why she can't see him. Rose, who is four and a half and used to sleep every night entwined with you, feels responsible. She confides to Susie that she wants to come and live with you in Cape Town, feeling that you need someone to look after you.

For the first few weeks, the girls cry every night. On top of my own grief, having to watch them in such pain is almost too much for me. I must survive for them. I'm all they've got. I do my best to reassure them that we are still a family, just a different kind. I remind them that the one thing that will never change is how much we both love them.

Susie says that Jane misses the bed-time stories the most and Rose misses your hugs and cuddles. So I do my best to compensate with regular stories and embraces. We introduce a new night-time routine to try and make bed time less sad. First, we each state three things that we are grateful for in our lives. Then we close our eyes and imagine sending you a strong beam of light that is full of love all the way from Durban to Cape Town; a light to surround you and keep you safe. The girls benefit from this and won't go to sleep without first going through the ritual.

During their sessions with Susie, Jane and Rose begin practicing visualization visits with you in their own secret imaginary place. They will often ask to visit their secret place before sleeping. I watch their faces as they do this; eyes tightly closed and mouths curling into a smile when they 'see' you. They then describe to me how they saw you running towards them; and how you hugged, talked, and laughed together. Susie has helped turn some of the bedtime tears into smiles and has given the girls a way to connect with you.

We start making plans to visit you in Cape Town in early January. Three months seem too long for the girls not to see you, but I need time to save money for the air tickets. Jane and Rose spend three days counting out a tin of silver coins we have collected. On the third day when young Rose gets tired, Jane scolds her for giving up too easily. She declares, "I'll never give up. I'm going to keep counting even though my back is sore and I'm tired. We must go and visit our Daddy because I love him!" Her dedication is shattering.

At night when the girls are asleep I sit alone on the stairs facing the house and smoking. The autumn wind rustles through the bamboo along each side of the stairway. This home was a refuge for both of us. Why did this all happen? One of the first things you told me after arriving in Cape Town was that you would never come back to Durban. Even though I try to comprehend that you are not in love with me, I still have faith that we will all be together again somehow. Once you've had some time away, perhaps it will become clear to you that you miss us terribly. Most importantly, I long for you to find your own happiness again and move away from misery. I reason that you will then either return home or we could move to Cape Town and make a fresh start. When I asked you to leave the house, I honestly thought you would move somewhere nearby and see us as much as possible. I whisper a plea to the wind to bring us back together, but I already know that it's not going to happen. It is too late. You have gone to a place of no return.

22

Following your move to Cape Town, your thoughts and emotions begin to unravel. Some days you appear to plausibly navigate the outward world but your inoperable internal wound is seeping toxin. You start to withdraw from everyone.

For a while, you stay in the guest room at Ruth and Bradley's house. It is some relief to know that you are in loving hands. I spend my days worrying and call as often as I can; but you hate the phone. The girl's voices make you more upset. Ruth and I keep in regular contact, monitoring your frame of mind.

Your withdrawal does not extend to messages, which I still receive several times a day. Each morning I rush to the computer and watch in dread as the send-and-receive line crosses in front of me. What message will it bring today? Your messages are seldom lighthearted and when one is, the next is sure to be a desperate one.

From: 'Stuart'
To: 'Robyn'
Sent: 21 October 2006 07:18 PM

You do know that I couldn't stay in Durban watching the two people I love get their lives together without me? I think I will survive here – I miss the girls so much and wonder if I even know how much yet.

And I worry about you. I don't know what the future will bring – at the moment, I don't really care.

I have heavy dreams and usually go to sleep and wake up crying. Don't tell Ruth – she is so sweet but can be a bit like my mother... dear thing. I try to be cheerful but there are visions everywhere and my emotional collapse while riding here is burned into my soul and I think I will be mad forever.

I miss Amanda. She phoned the other night – tearful. I am still in disbelief that all that is left unfinished will probably remain unfinished. I'm not angry with her – I just think love is one big disappointment and should be avoided or approached just above ground level, not elevated, open, reliant or expectant. I miss you, too, but, to be frank, worry more than miss because you have so much to weigh your soul down with, so much responsibility, so much sadness. I see reminders of "normality" everywhere and am hunted by myself. Which isn't much, so there's no threat.

xxx

To try and stay sane, I launch myself into tidying and rearranging the house. Spring cleaning is what I do when I feel something needs to be fixed; or I need to clear my head. At night after the girls go to sleep, I start by sorting through shelves and bookcases. Everywhere I look there are memories. Eight years of recollections. You took only a few clothes with you on the back of the motorbike; everything else is still here. I don't want anything to change too obviously for the girls' sake. I'm sure they don't believe that you are not coming home. To them, you have gone to stay with Ruth in Cape Town for a while to work. Maybe that's still what they believe or perhaps it is my hope. But I can't live in the house as I have for the past eight years and pretend that you will be back. This is my house now; I have to force myself to accept this.

I begin by going through all your books and CDs and packing your favorites neatly into boxes to send to you in Cape Town. Packing seems so final, but if I don't do it, I will be living in a strange place of in-between. Odd things make me cry, like seeing your scribbled name on the inside of your books or recognizing music that we all used to dance to when the girls were toddlers.

From: 'Stuart'
To: 'Robyn'
Sent: 01 November 2006 12:22 PM

Days like today, I don't think I will make it.

I feel where once I was a complicated and difficult to love person, I am now unfathomable and impossible to love.

I think all the time of what people can and can't do for and with each other; and I think of Amanda and hate myself and everyone else, the coldness and sex – how what people find easy and entertaining, I only find fearful and unavoidably painful.

I don't know what to say to the girls on the phone and I don't know what to do with my illness. I want to be as far away from everyone and everything as possible, just this side of death for the girl's sake.

Remember, Amanda wanted me gone, you wanted me gone; I am gone, and still feel it is right (fucked up right).

But I send you kind thoughts and love to the girls. x

From: 'Robyn'
To: 'Stuart'
Sent: 01 November 2006 01:06 PM

Stu, I will just say this – I never, ever wanted you gone. I did all I could and held on as long as I could to try and have it any other way. I wanted you here forever, you know that. Although I look at my decisions every day and live between doubt and strength, I think we did what was best for both of us. I know we will be close and am open to whatever the future may bring, but am living, as you are, for the day. You are lovable, but it has to start with you.

You despise yourself and therefore the world…
You do not feel loved without having someone to love you.
If that someone is not there, life seems not worth living.
I long for you to leave this difficult place you are in and find love.
I touch my forehead and think of you often.
You are loved, but not by yourself –
And in the end, that's the only one that counts.
xxx

23

Susie tells me that I need to find my anger; the anger that everyone thinks I should have, but I can't locate. Apparently I should feel anger towards you. I feel more hurt than angry. I'm wounded. If I had to be angry at something though, it would probably be your inability to make a choice. I feel that you have made selfish decisions; choices based on illusion rather than reality. I can't get my head around this one. I understand that feelings can change, but what about the girls? They adore you and you left them so easily. Now you are miserable in Cape Town, crying every day about a life you can't have with Amanda. We are here and have to keep ourselves laughing each day to get by. I am trying to find myself and my happiness because I love the girls and I want the best for them. But it is an effort. I am left with all this responsibility and keeping them safe; the pain of hearing them talk about you, answering their questions, trying to protect you. How do I explain to them how much you love them when you were prepared to leave? How does that make sense to a four-and-a-half year old who blames herself or to a heartbroken six year old? How do I continue to explain to Jane that she can't see her best friend anymore? This is what I deal with daily while you cry and I don't. These are the things that make me angry in a sad way. Some days I feel like I can't do this. Where is my partner, my husband; the man who promised to spend a lifetime with me? You are a thousand miles away and I am here. I am still here.

From: 'Stuart'
To: 'Robyn'
Sent: 28 November 2006 09:42 PM

I am lonely and want someone to talk to, but am crap on the phone; the things I would like to say to you would just be a babble of mumbles and futile attempts at trying to express myself.

Before sitting here at this computer, I turned the lights out and watched the neighbor's wife come home through the window, like a spy. She came in with a million shopping packets, he came and helped her carry them in; put them on the kitchen table. They didn't kiss; they unloaded shopping. I watched, waiting for them to touch each other in their kitchen. He went back to the outside room. And then I turn from the window in tears; these people, like so many others are dying, but doing what it means to live. They unpack the shopping; he is half naked, she doesn't run an affectionate finger across his chest, like a note, as they co-habit a very small space; no knowing glances or specialness.

Familiarity is worse than AIDs; its mortality rate is higher and has more severe effects than a predictable death. At least with death we know where we stand – with familiarity, boredom and biding time creeps up and kills that which we were born with and should carry forever. If I were to live with Amanda, would I help her unpack the shopping and then go back out to the back room to doodle on my guitar? Would she, coming in the door with packets, put them down on the table and touch my chest, kiss me, connect? Did we do this? Does anyone do this? I'm not suggesting that life is all about passion and sex; passion and sex is my weirdest enemy and ally – I live in a place of this and wonder what on earth to do with my physical, the limited time that we are given to walk around on this planet, do as the natural restraint demands. I am not mad – I know mad people and I am not one of them – but I fear I am cold because there is no room for my approach at warmth; I will be foolish, not with the program, an embarrassment. But, then, when two people are alone, naked in a room, without having to be afraid of each other, what rules apply?

When I left Durban, when Amanda and I met, we acknowledged our love is pure. Compared to what? Familiarity, sexual experimentation, shopping? And this is why I watch the neighbors through a darkened window.

I think that you and I, in our collective repression, are good friends because we share the same reticence, we prefer to meet as humans instead of mad people. But I want to meet as a madman; I think Amanda and I could live without day deaths. But there are children, the responsibility of being with the neediest man in the world, the threat that we actually couldn't. All I want is to live with her, love her. You will have much to say about that: she will fuck around, we will die. I am from another planet, so is she – not the same planet, but mutual aliens have an allegiance that is somehow stronger than these earthly bonds, it's just that reality is bigger than all of us and we are beaten; I am beaten because she still can spoon with her children. I spoon with a pillow.

I miss you tonight, but I don't miss you all the time. I'm not in love with you but am eternally grateful I know and have met you, that you are the person who carried our children, will be their mother. You have to know that I cannot thank you enough for you being who you are and being the mother of our children – who I miss with all my heart – they are in the same love and sex land that I physically have to turn my mind away from to prevent instant tears, such is how I miss them – but when I do think of them in purity, I sense the sky and the sea and this is why I am alive, why I suffer so much, why I hate shops and kisses and old people and lorries.

I am living a delusion – I think Amanda will come and live with me between now and death and we will suck this short experience dry. In moments of clarity, this doesn't go away.

But we are all beaten by reality; it is a common plague and I do not endorse it but am too scared to die on my own accord. I circle a black hole and the more I make efforts to be normal, the stranger I become; the stranger I become the more she is unsure about who I am, whether I am loveable. I fear being unlovable.

From: 'Robyn'
To: 'Stuart'
Sent: 29 November 2006 12:21 AM

I wish we could talk too. We can when I see you. Some thoughts in response to your letter…familiarity to me is wonderful, not death at all! This perhaps is where we differ so much, I could think of nothing better than spending my life with someone I love and am comfortable enough to have that familiarity with. The word familiarity does not conjure up thoughts of boredom or complacency to me but rather of words like comfortable, open, best friends, great sex, chats, honesty, and home. You're probably thinking – exactly, my worst! Yes and I think of old-age verandas, so what? That's what I want, that's what I dream of.

I also don't feel we have a limited time on this planet, although I'm not sure, I think we have many, many lifetimes to walk this planet, many lifetimes still to love and experience passion. I have no feeling of time running out, I feel like I am just beginning. You are not mad. You are not unlovable. There is so much room for all the love and warmth you have to give and you will have someone to give it to. If you want Amanda so much, start believing it will happen. For I still believe that whatever we want in this life, we can have. Possibility is always out there. Who knows what the future will bring? And there is time, so much time, for whichever way you look at it, life is short but it is also long. It may not be a complete delusion on your part. Anything could happen. I often think it might still too. I don't believe you would have the relationship you dream of with her, because reality is always there and can seem cruel as you see it. There are children and money hassles and shopping. I think there's a way to incorporate reality into love and passion, but that would involve familiarity.

In this and so many things, we see very differently. And that's okay. I hear your dreams and I understand them too. They are not as unrealistic as you may think. I know how much you miss the girls and love them. I know you are not in love with me. But I wish so much for them that you could somehow be a regular part of their lives. In this, I suppose, too, we don't know what the future will bring. I have no illusions though. But I have hope. On the one hand you speak of dreams and hopes and on the other you say you are beaten. Lean more towards the hopes if you can. Live with them. Beaten is not a nice way to walk through this life. You are strange, but not that strange. Those who love you will love you in spite of everything. You don't scare people and your strangeness is not something that people run away from, it is an attraction. If you could accept this and use it, embrace being different, talented, amazing, warm, loving, your perception of yourself will be the perception that others will have of you.

I miss you too and I look forward to seeing you, and we will see you as often as we can. I am so glad I know you and am grateful for this every day.

Sending love x

From: 'Stuart'
To: 'Robyn'
Sent: 30 November 2006 01:00 PM

I read this over and over. Perhaps I would not run from familiarity if it was with someone I love: but this is why I despise it when I see it around me, sense it far away; perhaps because I am jealous, because I don't have it and those that do take it for granted or abuse it or make it their everything or strangle it through need, not love. But your words are kind and positive and I am grateful for them. x

24

At the beginning of December 2006, after staying with Ruth for two months, you move into a tiny two-bedroom house of your own in the central suburb of Bo Kaap in Cape Town. Ruth and I worry more than ever that your depression will become even worse with only your own demons for companionship. She helps you move your few belongings and loans you colorful rugs, furniture and plants to try and make the place look like a home. You are worried about the expense, but reassure me that you will find a roommate in time. The money is my last concern; your sanity is my priority.

Susie suggests that I ask you to start writing letters to the girls as they are young and probably won't remember conversations. With letters, when they are older, they will have physical memories of your love. At my request, you surprise us with the letters that start arriving; beautiful pictures drawn for the girls. Jane is represented as a fairy and Rose, a mermaid. You write them poems and send dried flowers. The girls paste the letters up next to the bed and read them every night. I get a letter from you too.

1 December 2006

My dearest Robyn

One of the things that pains me the most is having deserted you as a support to your fragile self-confidence. That it is possible to wade past love and passion is debatable, but to have left a soul un-tethered is unforgivable, and I need to be forgiven for this, somehow, although I accept it not happening despite your pure alignment to the light and positivity. Your dreams of companionable lifetimes are enviable and worthy; that I have let you down in this is hard for me, harder for you. But you must know that I haven't gone completely – we are mutual DNA collaborators of our beautiful children and we know each other so well (do we?) – well enough to know that our bond is stronger than our fears, and this is a comfort to me, and I hope to you too.

I will never be far away from you and the girls and everything I do in reality – trying to make your life as easy as possible (!) I will do; if I win a million bucks, it's all yours; if I have one fridge thought in my lap, I transfer it to you. But I fear I will be useless and if you think you've married into a rich family that is backed up by inheritance, I wouldn't be so sure. Your folks are a better bet, if you think like this. I see a future of hardship with little prospects (until I get translated into sixteen languages for my first novel…?).

Your visualization works for you and I look at this with some wonder and admiration. You wily little gypsy you! I want you to stick to your spirit and ignore every ridicule I've laid upon you before; you are right, I am uncertain. If, in amongst the crowded rooms of your dreams, you have a spare nook for visualizing (!) happiness, take it for yourself, challenge your needs and ego with what your soul and body requires – you always say you are 'on hold' or something – it would make my heart sing to know that yours is singing too, without me as an albatross. It is a challenge because I know how you protect yourself but you don't need protection, your soul is pure and need never be shameful, do not be pressured by the fridge-world – your geography is superior to theirs and you are a teacher that cuts through the norms to a place of compassion and tenderness, excitement and fun.

We are just too similar for each other, my gentle friend. We would wait forever for something to happen instead of being in a place where things do happen. And I am convinced that when things do happen, a whole new life unfolds where sadness becomes a memory and each dawn is a blessing and the lonesome hours are spent in color instead of black and white.

I am so happy we met; I am so confused about the next levels, which I believe exist. I am frightened about leaving this level – there is so much! – but know we must press on, even if it all turns out tits-up, which it won't if we are forever close, which I know we will be.

Your ear is the most valuable port for my words, knowing that you are with dear Jane and Rose, that you live with your heart, do the best you can with the world and try to live without anger and bitterness, such human emotions. Perhaps out of similarity, you can vent these things in a realm of real fridge-love (where passion is matched by needs) and become even stronger than you are now... your own record company, mirrors above the bed...

Of mirrors – you know better than I that it is futile to expect other people to be mirrors of one's self. We are not mirrors to each other and this is good. This is why we can live forever on this planet together as we do. Thank you.

But mirrors are everything if you're unstable. These are the relationships that make the stars brittle and the days short and long. Dad and I are mirrors. Amanda and I are mirrors, Spooks and I were mirrors, and Rose and I are mirrors. This is my world; all the mumbo-jumbo of healing will not change this; the fridge-world will never claim us, the essence is in the reflection and its intensity will never die. Love is hard here – one's own warts are those of your neighbors, one's own heavens are the others' joys. Perilous, dangerous, perhaps, but for the half-mad, this is where it all happens – what the fridge-world does is deplorable, rudimentary, and enviable; deserving of a wary distance and an alarming respect at the lightness and ease at how they engage – words, bodies, dreams, and reality; fantastic. They will be forever the yardstick of my failings, the catalyst of my actions.

One day, I will love as a fridge-man and turn over in my mind, without ruffling the sheets. Until then, I live in a twilight zone of anxiety and know that whatever happens, I will never be far from your side and will always be right next to our monkeys.

Love Stu

I sit outside on the veranda with coffee and read your letter several times; trying to make sense of where you are, what you are thinking. Your letters are often in contrast with your e-mail messages. You recently e-mailed me about the two herons at the Durban harbor. When you were still here, you often spoke of the pair of herons that lived on the water's edge. You told me that when you used to go down to play your accordion at the docks alone, there was often just one heron there. If you were there with Amanda, there were always two. Although I've never seen them, I imagine the pair of herons with their long necks and unblinking yellow eyes wading in the shallows of the ocean; their gray feathers shining with droplets in the moonlight. What do these herons represent? To me, they hold the reminder of that last secret kiss; the kiss that let me know that you will never be free of her.

When it comes to you and me, there are no herons. The only bird you speak of is an albatross. You have often said that you are an albatross around my neck. Even though I didn't know what you meant, I assured you that you were not.

I research the albatross and find that it is a great big seabird and that you are referring to a poem. In the poem, an albatross is following a ship which is seen as a sign of good luck. A mariner shoots the albatross and is made to wear the bird around his neck as a punishment by his shipmates. The albatross is a burden. The other sailors all die from the curse. The mariner, alone, sees a vision and offers a prayer, after which the albatross falls off his neck into the sea.

25

Since you left home I have been continually sick with colds and flu. You say you are drowning in silence. I am drowning in my own phlegm. My body is not able to cope with all the emotional stress. Now it has gone to my chest. A pain grips my lungs and bleeds into my stomach and shoulders. Breathing and laughing are difficult. Not that I feel much like laughing. Sleep is almost impossible. I have to prop myself upright so that I can avoid choking. The doctor says it's bronchial and I need another course of antibiotics. I keep chain smoking.

From: 'Stuart'
To: 'Robyn'
Sent: 11 December 2006 09:30 AM

My nights are so heavy, Robyn; so much time to think and so alone – I don't think I'm going to make it. I don't know what to do with myself; I cry all the time and can't sleep. I'm tired of being sick. Am still not angry with Amanda – as she once said to me: 'love is generous,' which implied that there is something wrong with me, as I would say to her now, holed up with her family and safety. I can't come back to you, everything's changed and at the moment I don't feel like being here either and I see a life of bad things ahead and hope it doesn't last too long; I've had enough. Love the girls x

I'm losing ground. I am not sure what to do. I call Ruth. She is doing all she can. Some nights she insists on sleeping at your house, even though you bark at her to leave you alone.

Just when it sounds like you are feeling better, I get another fraught message from you. I am not sure exactly what I am dealing with. I need to get to Cape Town. We have booked tickets for the beginning of January, but that's a month away. It's too long. Changing the tickets would cost money that we don't have. I have to hold on; it seems there is nothing else I can do.

Ruth and Bradley are away for the weekend when you phone me one Saturday night. I can barely make out what you are saying but understand that you had gone into the sea and swam out as far as you could go. All I can get through your sobs is "But it was too cold, Robyn, so cold, so cold and dark…I was so scared."

As you calm down, I listen in alarm as you explain how you cleared all the documents off your computer and planned to swim out to sea and never return. You mention that you recently asked Amanda on the phone to reassure you that everything was going to be okay. But she couldn't do it; stating that she didn't know that for sure. I try to convince you now that I do know; I know everything is going to be okay.

"Please hold on Stu. The girls and I will be down soon."

I beg you to hang in for your girls. Through your tears you murmur, "I love you Robyn, you know that don't you?"

"Yes, I know."

You can't speak anymore so I suggest you try and get some sleep and I'll talk to you soon. I'll see you soon. If only Ruth were in town, I could call her to come and stay with you. Despite all your threats and the fact that you've been into the sea before, this time is more terrifying. You don't have the girls and me nearby and your state of being has deteriorated. We should be there.

The necessity of updating our last will and testaments

becomes a priority. I contact a funeral parlor in Cape Town about your prior request for a burial at sea and on investigation, I find that although this is legal in South Africa, it is a complicated and expensive process. After discussing this with you, I make the necessary edits to the existing documents and post them for your approval and signature. The courier delivers it back to me with the following inserted paragraph –

"It is my desire that upon my death my whole remains shall be buried at sea, the place to be determined by my wife, failing which, my sister, Ruth. If this proves to be too costly, then a routine cremation will suffice and my ashes deposited into a rubbish bin on any street in any town. It is my express desire that under no circumstances will a funeral or memorial service be held for me, however, should friends choose to get pissed together somewhere, then the songs Moon River and Squeeze's Vicky Verky would be appropriate to play once everyone is soused."

26

Ruth has resumed her daily commitment as your guardian, keeping a closer eye on you than usual. But Christmas is coming and you are going to be on your own. Ruth and Bradley will be visiting us and we will be spending Christmas with your family. No amount of begging would get you to consider coming back to Durban, even for the holidays. You scoff at Christmas but we still receive a parcel in the post from you; a gift for the girls. They open it in anticipation and look slightly disappointed. But I know that it is perfect; beautiful. I understand how long it must have taken to make and how you would have threaded each bead with care. In years to come this gift will be better than any Barbie or Lego or plastic toy. Two handmade necklaces; beaded words and pendants threaded carefully onto thin wire and closed neatly with a clasp. On them, with intricate beading in between are the words: SUN – MOON – STARS – SEA.

A few days before Christmas you send me a message saying that I must stop sending your belongings down to Cape Town; you don't need anything. I ignore this and continue to pack boxes to bring to you, refusing to acknowledge that you might not be around to need them. Your messages continue to be as perturbing as ever. Christmas is meaningless under the circumstances. Still, I make an extra effort to look enthusiastic for the girls. I'm living two entirely different realities.

From: 'Stuart'
To: 'Robyn'
Sent: 23 December 2006 12:53 PM

I need to hear from Amanda, from her alone, her words of comfort. I need to hold her have her near, I'm not going to make it and don't think you should come here. I had to go home at 1p.m. yesterday because I was going to break down in the office. I need her. I think of death all the time, this world I have become a part of is unlivable. I disgust myself, my spotty body, my horrible face. I've had it but am so afraid of crossing the line, leaving damage and pain behind but can't stay here, having her near would make the only change, I would be normal, would love the girls.

From: 'Stuart'
To: 'Robyn'
Sent: 23 December 2006 03:12 PM

Sorry for the fraught message, just need to speak. I think I'll take up drinking again, the emotional maelstrom is better than having to be in touch with reality. love the girls.

From: 'Robyn'
To: 'Stuart'
Sent: 23 December 2006 05:20 PM

My dearest Stu

I wish I could help you, I don't know what to say; my words are meaningless. I remember you saying that Amanda couldn't even tell you that everything was going to be alright. Jane has just left another message for you. Try to find comfort from their love, which is so real, so pure. Your house, your girls, your life, your body, your face, your surroundings... all will become beautiful only when it is loved by you. Beauty is in the eye of the beholder. I hope for the day when you can look around and find that beauty and that love and realize that it all had nothing to do with her, she just unlocked something in you, which you now have to take further on your own. Being alone, something you fear is your greatest challenge. I suppose my positive words irritate you sometimes. When you are at the bottom of your black hole, look around and carefully size up the options. There are options, choices. And make one. All the time, remember the two little people who will always be part of your life. Keep busy, small steps my friend. x

From: 'Stuart'
To: 'Robyn'
Sent: 23 December 2006 08:18 PM

Sorry – I really appreciate your words; you know how I fuck out when alienated and your contact is valued. I love the girls so much, they make me bleed inside. x

From: 'Stuart'
To: 'Robyn'
Sent: 27 December 2006 11:58 AM

Was late for work, went to the sea at dawn. I am so afraid, there was seaweed near the bottom and I just need Amanda more than anything, and now I am at work trying to be normal. I need her and love her more than life and I don't know how to deal with her going further away, I chase into nothing and don't know where she is or what she thinks. I just don't know what to do, what I can do. Time and baby steps and all that is useless, I need her near, that's all.

From: 'Stuart'
To: 'Robyn'
Sent: 27 December 2006 03:50 PM

Sorry for (another) fraught mail this morning... Am having a terrible time, gutted by longing and disbelief. Hope you are okay – don't worry about me, will muddle on; love the girls.

Time can't move fast enough. Ruth is on her way back to Cape Town after Christmas, thank god, and we will be there in a week. I have no intention of not coming as you suggested. In the meantime, a friend has invited us to go camping in the mountains with her family over New Year. I accept because it will help pass time and will be enjoyable for the girls. It is only when we are making final arrangements that I discover that we are going to be camping at the same location where you spent that dreadful week in March; the place where Amanda came to you.

The three days at the camp site pass slowly. We walk across the swinging wooden bridge where I remember that you and Amanda sat drinking red wine. The girls pick wild apples to feed to the horses. We take long walks to waterfalls and swim in icy pools; the same pools where you told me you had planned to drop to the depths if Amanda hadn't come. The girls and I balance river stones into cairns. We toss gratitude pebbles into the river and collect smooth brown acorns to bring to you. Through all this I am not present; I can't wait to get on the plane. On New Year's Eve it rains so hard I wonder if our tent will withstand it. I wonder if I will survive this.

From: 'Stuart'
To: 'Robyn'
Sent: 03 January 2007 09:20AM

Looking forward to seeing you and the girls. Will have to do some shopping; have nothing in the house. Can you ask your doctor for a week or so worth of industrial-strength sleeping pills... I succumb. I don't sleep anyway (look like a scarecrow) and am fearful of when you leave and will just want to sleep at night instead of doing my head in. Please.

Will see you at the airport tomorrow! x

27

Your new house is situated in the Bo Kaap in Cape Town, a vibrant multicultural district above the city center tucked into the fold of Signal Hill. The steep and narrow cobble stoned streets are lined with tiny brightly-colored Malay houses from as far back as the seventeenth century. The girls open the small wrought-iron gate and run inside to explore. It makes me happy that you have your own veranda; which you refer to in typical Bo Kaap Afrikaans as your *stoep*. On the veranda are two worn gray sofa chairs. Throughout the house I recognize Ruth's warm touches, unmistakably sprinkled in the combination of borrowed furniture, potted plants, and colorful rugs.

Two items I carry heavily in my bag are the prescription sleeping tablets that you asked for and a digital camera, which I borrowed for this trip. I am horribly aware that this may be my last opportunity to take photographs of you with the girls. They can't grow up without remembering you. Photographs can prove that you were here; that you were with them and that you loved them.

Ruth has lent us her car and you have taken the week off work. Each morning we pack a day bag and head off to a new area of Cape Town to explore. We visit the penguins in Simonstown, the seals in Hout Bay and feed the squirrels in the Company Gardens. In Kalk Bay, we collect seashells, glass, and pebbles and paddle in the ocean. A walk down the hill from your house takes us to Long Street in the city center, where we spend hours exploring the shops crammed with hidden treasures and secondhand book stores; drinking cappuccinos in ambient coffee bars. In Cape Town, even the people seem colorful and unique. I take as many photographs as I can without making it too obvious.

Through all this excitement and fun, your dialogue is limited to chatter with the girls. Each night you lie in bed and tell them bedtime stories while stroking their hair and gently kissing their foreheads. Then you sink into your gray chair next to me on the veranda in silence. My futile attempts at communication are met with a grunt or an upward nod. By the third day, I am so craving conversation that I invite Ruth and Bradley for dinner. After they leave, I am left with yet another night of silence in the colorful Bo Kaap and another monologue. I talk about the pigeons that nest in the roof across the road and how all the stray neighborhood cats seem to be gingers. I comment on the tramps and the way the mountain makes a shadow on the buildings. I speak of the sea and how I love the way the sun sets so late in Cape Town. Spinning tales of life back home in Durban, and the girls' silly sayings and notable achievements, I do my best to talk about anything under that late Cape Town sun. At some point, I run out of things to say. When I stare at you and ask why you are speechless, your one sentence answer is the only thing you say all night, "There is nothing to talk about."

For the whole week, I persevere in the hope that things will change, that it will be possible for us to be like old friends again. But nothing changes. There is small talk around the girls during the day and agonizing nothingness once they go to bed at night. At a certain point, I stop talking. I have absolutely nothing left to speak about. Instead, I begin to look at my surroundings and listen to the sounds of the street. Across the road is a building that houses the Zimbabwean workers of a local hotel and I watch their shadows behind closed curtains. I note what time the sun goes down and where the light lands on the mountain. Counting how many cigarettes I can smoke in an hour of quiet and observing how the same man walks past every night at almost the same time. The Cape Malay curry smells entertain me, and I count how many children live next door and what time they go to bed. From time to time I try another opening line, something as fascinating as I can muster up after having hours to think about it. It is always met with the same blankness.

On our second last night in Cape Town, after the lights are turned out, I signal to you to join me in my futon bed on the floor. You hesitate but come. I am desperate for some form of contact with you. Strained lovemaking was the closest I got, and although you didn't say anything, you cried.

On our last evening, you indicate that you won't be able to drive us to the airport, it will be too unbearable for you to say goodbye to the girls. You ask for the sleeping tablets so that you can sleep after we've gone. I count out fourteen, enough for two weeks, even though I have more. In the morning, Ruth arrives to collect us. On the hot pavement outside your house, you nod a quick goodbye to me while packing our suitcases into the car. Then kneeling down you hold the girls tightly and with a strange gasp in your throat you remind them that you love them more than the sun, the moon, the stars, and the sea before running inside and quickly shutting the door. I know that you are weeping and for a moment, I consider staying. Forgetting about my flight and my life; my business, house and pets. Still, I drag myself into the car because I have to and we drive further and further away from you. I picture you on your bed, a terribly lonely image, and then later tidying up all the items the girls left strewn around your house; shells and pictures and sand. The images are devastating.

In the car, Rose casually mentions that you promised her that if anything happens to you and you die that you will never really leave her; she must just look up to the rabbit in the moon and know that you still love her. Ruth and I give each other terrified glances. At the airport, I watch Ruth's red car ride away and force myself to keep moving. My tears flow uncontrollably as I wait in the check-in queue. How can I leave? How can I take the girls away, knowing that they may never see you again? I consider turning around, phoning Ruth to come back. I can't go home. I can't leave. But I have responsibilities. I can't stay.

28

Responsibilities. There is a mound of things to be done at home. E-mails, piles of mail, admin of the studio, phone calls, housework, groceries, pets... It's all too much and I can't seem to focus on any of it. Instead I decide to paint the lounge walls; a meditative nothingness. I choose magenta and orange. It keeps my mind off everything I dread; the things I can't think about. The strokes of the paintbrush, up and down, keep me sane. That's all. I also do my best to love the girls as much as possible, like you asked. Nothing else feels important. I sometimes don't brush my teeth or bathe for up to two days at a time. I can't get anything together, except painting and reading to the girls.

Jane and Rose were sad to leave you, but as far as they are concerned, we will be going back in a few months time to have another fun-filled holiday. I've promised them that we will go to Cape Town every three months if we can afford it. At the same time, inwardly, I struggle not to give any credibility to my fear that you may not be around in three month's time.

At night I fall into bed in my clothes, with my bra still on, and have to remind myself consciously to unclench my hands and my jaw. I fall asleep with worry and wake up with a feeling of dread; rushing straight to my computer to see what word it brings from you. Your silence, thankfully, does not carry on with your messages. At the very least they mean that you are still there. On the odd occasion, you sound slightly cheery and hope rises momentarily, but the next moment you feel tired and sad and disgusted with everything. One thing is certain, seeing your name in my inbox, no matter what it brings, is better than not hearing from you and what that means.

From: 'Stuart'
To: 'Robyn'
Sent: 10 January 2007 04:50 PM

I am afraid, I don't want to be here – but the girls.

I hate myself and this world and its people, I can't believe I'll never see or hold Amanda again, that she is the most extraordinary thing that has happened to me and she has let me down, has what she needs. I don't hate her; I love her more.

Will you update that life insurance thing – be practical and love yourself; you are lovely, love the girls. I will be okay but just as a practical measure. Hope you are okay, the house is not too smelly, the studio works and the girls are alright. x

---

From: 'Stuart'
To: 'Robyn'
Sent: 13 January 2007 04:22 PM

Hung over – feeling panicky today. Messaged Amanda asking

her to call if she can but I don't think she will...

It is quiet at work and I am writing myself a porn fantasy story to try to make up for the hole in my middle.

From: 'Stuart'
To: 'Robyn'
Sent: 15 January 2007 11:31 AM

Hello. hope you are well – am in a good mood today, maybe because I've entered a new reality after a week of cheap whisky every night...

I want you to be happy, my friend, mother of our children. I send warm thoughts, caring thoughts.

x

From: 'Stuart'
To: 'Robyn'
Sent: 17 January 2007 04:06 PM

I am pining; haven't heard from Amanda

From: 'Stuart'
To: 'Robyn'
Sent: 18 January 2007 09:46 AM

hung over again...

it rains here today, the first time in ages and I could very easily sit in a cafe all day reading, dreaming.

hope you are okay.

x

From: 'Stuart'
To: 'Robyn'
Sent: 18 January 2007 05:13 PM

I'm hung over (again) – took huge leaps of faith today – I am so lonely – and asked two people from work to go for coffee: "am in a relationship," and "too tired." I feel humiliated and alienated. Fuck them all, I am an old fart with scary eyes and bitten nails. It's all bollocks, I am tired and disgusted.

From: 'Robyn'
To: 'Stuart'
Sent: 19 January 2007 3:48 PM

I was having this daydream today of building a second storey on the outside room with a tiny little staircase leading up… it was of course only if you ever decided to come back…

Other daydreams include, me moving the entire studio to Cape Town (and the house), it's not that I am thinking of us getting back together, but I just hate being so far away from you! x

---

From: 'Stuart'
To: 'Robyn'
Sent: 19 January 2007 03:59 PM

I am so tired, have been trashed every night for two weeks and am beginning to feel it. I'm just down the road. Don't do the 'if only' and 'what if' thing. I will be dead in a year, anyway.

29

I have finished painting and I'm spring cleaning again; another way to try and pass through this nightmare without living it. Your messages become worse; you're not going to get through this. Your birthday is in a week's time and I'm uneasy. You loathe the thought of getting old. I urge Susie to help me find an alternative method to help you. I have read about the possibility of standing proxy for someone in alternative healing therapies, psychic even, anything. If you won't go, I could do it for you. Ruth and I have continued to plead with you to seek professional help, but you point-blank refused. Susie suggests that we could use the pendulum if I bring in a photograph of you. I meet her with the photograph and a lock of your baby hair. The answers we obtain via the pendulum suggest that your struggle started due to circumstances when you were four years old. I am suspicious and rephrase the questions again. We get the same clear response. The next day, I meet your parents for lunch and start casually trying to find out more about you at the age of four. Your father finally enquires why I am doing all of this. I look at him clearly as I say, "To try and save a life."

His response is that he has known you your entire existence. He guarantees that you will never take your own life. All I can murmur is, "I hope you are right."

Gita is a new friend of mine. She is fun and crazy and also happens to be a spiritual counselor and art therapist. We met at one of her Mandala painting classes. Tonight I am at her house drinking rum and apple juice; it's all she has. Gita doesn't drink but she smokes hand-rolled cigarettes made from herbal tea leaves in an attempt to give up tobacco. She makes me laugh and that is something I desperately need now.

As the night progresses I ask Gita to shave off all my hair. For most my life, I have had long black hair. My mother used to tell me that my thick dark curls were my crowning glory. The only time I ever cut it short was soon after you and I got married. It was something I had often wanted to try, but was too afraid that I might lose my beauty and become ugly. When I finally found someone who loved me enough, I took the plunge. It looked okay but I let it grow again. Now, eight years later, I want it all gone. In some strange form of a ritual, I need to prove to myself that there are some things that don't matter; things less valuable than a life. Gita is daring enough to shave it all off for me, leaving less than a centimeter all over. I feel oddly free.

The week leading up to your birthday is incredibly tough. I ask you about your childhood but you can't remember anything from four years old. You get quieter and more withdrawn. Your home phone has stopped working and you say there is no reason to fix it. Your motorbike is in for repairs and you make no attempt to collect it. You tell me how much you will be earning at the end of the month and ask me to make sure that you get paid. Your salary still comes into my bank account. I have always been in charge of the finances.

On Wednesday night, I turn out the lights at the usual two a.m. Out of nowhere I start howling into my pillow. From the pit of my being I cry for you, as if it is the last time. The next day I feel uncomfortable. I try to speak to you but you don't want to talk. On Friday 26th January, your birthday, I message you several times at work and get no reply. That evening I call Susie after hours, something I've never done. I explain to her that today you turned thirty-nine years old and I have a dreadful feeling about this weekend. I ask Susie to hold you close and pray or whatever it is she does because you need it now. On Saturday night before you leave work for the weekend, I finally receive a message from you.

From: 'Stuart'
To: 'Robyn'
Sent: 27 January 2007 08:15 PM

You do know that I care about you and the girls very much, don't you? Never forget that. Love them doubly. I just want you and the girls to be okay, whatever happens.

It has been so hot here the past few days – up to 40C! I sleep naked on a sheet and in the morning, it and the pillows are like stew. Did you get my recent letter? I can't really remember what the fine details were but there were some things I think were important in there. Everything about people and how they live inside and outside themselves makes me cry. The accordion in its case knows everything.

PART IV

30

On Sunday morning my phone rings and a strange voice says, "This is the Cape Town Medical and Rescue Services. Do you know someone by the name of Stuart?"

My stomach plummets as I meekly reply, "Yes, he's my husband."

The voice continues, "There's been an accident."

It is two days after your thirty-ninth birthday. The late morning light filters through the trees and flickers onto the veranda where I'm drinking coffee in my pajamas. I am unaware of the letter that lays waiting in my mailbox. I sit down and begin to tremble. This is the call that I have been expecting but hoped I would never get.

I listen, just wanting to hear you that are alright. The man on the other end of the phone gently explains that you are unconscious after nearly drowning in a mountain dam. He guesses you may have had an epileptic fit. The rescue team is trying to get you down the mountain on a stretcher to the ambulance. He tells me that he called my number because it was the first one listed in the diary he found in your back pack, which you had left near the dam.

The rescue worker cannot guarantee me that you will make it. I manage to punch in your sister Ruth's number. She is expecting a call too. Ruth was suspicious when you arrived at her house early this morning to borrow her bicycle. Her unsettled feeling was due less to the manic way you were behaving and more to the way you kissed her goodbye. Ruth and Bradley jump into the car while I am still talking; on their way to you. Shaking violently, I book the first available air tickets to Cape Town. I can't think straight. I have to make it to you on time. Please, please be okay.

There's an hour to get to the airport. In a calm voice, I urge the girls to get dressed; we are going to Cape Town. Dad has had a swimming accident. I throw a few clothes into a suitcase, feed the animals, call the pet sitter, and leave home. Ruth and I stay in phone contact. The medical workers take some time getting you to the ambulance and then stabilizing you. Ruth tells me that you were pulled off the bottom of the dam by an onlooker who saw you struggling and then sinking. Just before I get onto the plane, you are being rushed to the hospital with Ruth and Bradley chasing closely behind. You are still unconscious. I don't know if I will see you again alive. It's an excruciating two-hour flight with no phone contact. I just want to be with you, to cling to you and let you know that it's all okay.

Bradley takes us directly to the hospital from the airport where Ruth is pacing. It's been a traumatic day for her, and so I take over. The girls go home with Ruth and Bradley and I am left in the strange hospital alone.

I tiptoe into the dimly lit intensive care unit, wash my hands and introduce myself to the nurses. They point me to your bed where you are on life support. You are in a coma, but you are alive. Alive. I kiss you lightly and sit down to stare at you. Is this a suicide attempt as I suspect or did you have a serious accident? The green lines on the computer screen go up and down. A machine is breathing for you with a terrifying wheezing sound, pumping air in and out of your lungs through a tube taped into your mouth. Your hands are tied to the sides of the bed so that you can't pull out the tubes as you thrash around moaning. I take your hand. There is no response.

There are so many thoughts; so many days, weeks, years of thoughts. I am sure of only one thing. I love you. If only I could scoop you up. I'd whip you out of this hospital and take you back to Durban; back to our home. I would make all of this go away and keep you safe. I put my lips to your ear and whisper, "Everything's going to be okay Stu. I am here now. It's okay. I love you." I ask you to squeeze my hand if you can hear me and I am surprised that you do.

The rest of the evening I spend between your bedside and running down to the smoking room to smoke and to speak with Susie. I also have to deal with phone messages from concerned family and friends.

When the nurse comes over to speak to me, she questions me about your blood test results, which have come back positive for recreational drugs. I shake my head. You use drugs only if they are offered to you at a party, never having enough money to buy them yourself. As far as I know, you haven't taken any in quite a while. I know this because I monitor the amount of money I put into your account. I make sure that there is just enough for basic expenses and not enough for extras, given your current state of mind. I ask whether it could be sleeping tablets and she answers a definite no. At this stage, she explains that she doesn't know if you will be brain damaged yet. I ask for your sedation to be upped as you seem too restless. Only once I'm sure you are safe and still, around midnight, do I call Ruth to fetch me and take me to her house so I can sleep with the girls.

I catch a taxi back to the hospital at 6 a.m. After I've had my first cigarette, you start showing signs of coming around. Your eyes flicker and roll back and then you open them wide and look directly at me. There is no way you can talk because you have too many tubes and the tape holding them in place is also taping your mouth closed. Various thoughts seem to move through your eyes: first terror, then surprise, then shock and fear. None of them are of anything resembling relief. I assume that you are trying to work out where you are. If this is heaven with all the bright white lights, why am I here grinning at you? This is the first time you've seen me with my shaved head and it must be an alarming sight.

I come close to explain, "Stu, there was an accident at the dam. You nearly drowned but someone managed to save you. You were brought to the hospital yesterday and you are in intensive care."

Your eyes get bigger. Then you narrow them and stare ahead. I sit down again and take your hand and you clasp mine. For a while you slip in and out of sleep. Then you start struggling with the tubes and frowning, frantically trying to communicate something with your head and eyes. I prop you up, and then lie you down, but nothing seems to help and, chuckling a little, I apologize for never having been skilled at charades. I finally understand that you want the tubes removed. The nurse on duty threatens to tie your hands down again. In a gentle voice I tell you that I know how much you hate hospitals, but if you fight, you'll only make things worse for yourself.

At last the doctor does his rounds and says you can be set free of all the machines. When the nurses finally get everything out of your mouth, you try to speak but have no voice, no whisper even and your lips are floppy. I put my ear on your mouth to make out your frustrated splutter, "What am I doing here?"

Patiently I repeat what I said before and then ask you if it was an accident. I don't want to speculate before hearing your story. You nod. Relief washes over my tired body but vanishes again a moment later as you beckon me closer. With a hoarse breathiness in my ear you declare, "No, but you can't tell anyone." I move my head slowly up and down in non-committal agreement. You add that you took 100 sleeping tablets before swimming out into the dam.

Most of the morning is spent in silence except for the pumping and squeezing and beeping of other patient's machines. You erratically wheeze questions into my ear. How did I get here? Where is Ruth? Where are the girls? When I ask why you did this in the middle of a Sunday morning at a family outing spot you assert that there was no one around. I tell you that some guy having a picnic saw you waving your arms around and drowning, that he jumped in to save you. Your only comment is, "Bastard."

When the doctor does the lunch-time rounds, he says you are ready to move to a general ward and that a psychiatrist will be visiting you there. As soon as they wheel you to the new ward, you start planning your getaway; claiming you are not staying in this place. You look for your clothes even though you aren't yet strong enough to walk. I am quite desperate for you to stay one more night for observation after being unconscious, and so that you can see the psychiatrist. But you will not hear of it. As you sign yourself out of the hospital I speak in hushed tones to the sister on duty, pleading for her to find a way to force you to stay. She says she can't; you are free to go, this is not a psychiatric hospital. It seems there is nothing I can do about it right now. So I call a taxi and push you outside in a wheel chair.

31

Ruth is furious that you have signed yourself out of hospital before seeing the psychiatrist. You go and lie down in the guest room and cuddle up with the girls. I inform Ruth of all that happened as we drink coffee and smoke outside. Ruth calls your father to implore him to come to Cape Town to help us. After a nap you join us in the garden for tea and in a voiceless whisper give us more information. You had planned the day carefully and are extremely disappointed with the outcome. You borrowed Ruth's bicycle and cycled for miles up to the dam. You knew what you were going to do and described it as the most peaceful day of your life. Sitting next to the water, you smoked your last cigarette. After swallowing a hundred sleeping pills, you did a final check to make sure everything would look like an accident. The last thing you remembered was swimming out into the crystal clear water. You say that you are no longer scared of dying, that there was nothing scary about it. Living is the scary thing.

The blood test results are a mystery to all of us. You had not taken any recreational drugs. When you are not looking, Ruth packs away all knives, razors and other sharp objects and locks them in her car. After you go to sleep I collect all the door keys and hide them so you can't run away during the night.

The following morning your father arrives, to your astonishment. You have always held a special connection with him. He reminds me of you in many ways with his wild hair, piercing blue eyes, love of music and hatred of doctors. Since the time you were in the army though, you made a point of distancing yourself from your family. Your parents came into money after you left home and you seemed to hold this against them as though they now represented a part of the fridge-world. I have been the one who makes an effort to encourage a relationship. Sitting outside in the garden, Ruth, your father, and I try to convince you to seek help; see a psychiatrist, and get medication for depression. You don't speak. You still have no voice and besides, I know you have nothing to say. I think you are still in shock at how it all went wrong. After making such an effort, you had still buggered it up. I sense you are very angry; angry with yourself and angry with the man who saved you. Your father does his best to offer you support and again, asks you to see a doctor. Ruth starts to say something and I begin to cry. Self-conscious, I turn to you and say, "Please, Stu. Do you know what it's like for us to go to bed every night wondering if you're okay and wake up every morning waiting to hear from you? We can't do it anymore. Please see someone."

To all of our surprise, you consent. Ruth books the first appointment we can get with a recommended psychiatrist which is for a week later. A week?! We clarify that this is an emergency; a suicide attempt. But they apologize and state that this is the earliest appointment they have available.

After your father leaves to fly home, you tell Ruth and me that you will do it again. It might not happen right away; it could be a month or a year, but you will try again.

Because you have no voice, you ask Ruth to call Amanda to let her know what has happened. Amanda is undoubtedly shocked and spends the next few days worrying and phoning Ruth for frequent updates.

Promising that you won't do anything stupid, you fetch your motorbike from the repair shop and plan a road trip; claiming you need space from Ruth and me as we are too stifling. There is nothing we can do to stop you and so we wait in trepidation for three days until you arrive back at Ruth's house safely, skillfully missing your first agreed psychiatric appointment.

All this time, I look after the girls and pray for a miracle. The girls think that you had an accident and are okay now. Your motorbike trip was to Cape Aghulas, the southernmost tip of Africa and you bring the girls each back a pebble, telling them it's from the end of the world.

While you were away, a package had arrived from Amanda in

the mail and when you open it, we see that it includes some tea tree oils and creams and a short note that says – 'Dearest Stu, I am holding you close. I really, really miss you.' I feel a little annoyed at the gesture. How? And by this I mean how on earth is tea tree oil going to help you now? But I try not to be critical. We are all doing our best. While you are hiding out in the spare room, I spend hours on the Internet researching suicide and depression. I make several phone calls to private psychiatric hospitals to find out if they will take you against your will. They won't. Apparently you have to book yourself in. No chance of that. I keep phoning, hoping to find someone who can help. No one can. Everyone I speak to is kind, but their advice is unhelpful to the circumstances. It seems that without you wanting to help yourself, there is little we can do. I feel lost.

You decide to go back to your house in the Bo Kaap and so the girls and I come to stay with you there. You and I spend the evenings talking on your veranda about living and dying and what you are thinking. None of it is very encouraging. You say that you've had a great life, done everything you want to do and that from now on, it will only be downhill. It will all lead to depravity. You think you are destined for this. I beg you to reconsider, if not for yourself, then for your girls. You are such a wonderful dad and the girls are too young to remember you. To that you reply, "Well then, you'll just have to remind them."

We make love a couple of times. Holding your bony, naked body is almost too unbearable for me; touching it and knowing that it could have been lifeless, dead. You keep inquiring as to when we are going home. Each time I answer that I won't leave you like this. I can't walk away this time and watch you and the girls saying goodbye. I'll go when I know you are alright. I suspect you then start to put on a bit of an act, pretending to be fine. We plan our next trip to Cape Town for March. You return to work and seem more comfortable. So against my better judgment, I book air tickets home. We've been in Cape Town for ten days and I am thankful the girls have had this extra time with you. You take them for walks to the museum and to the towering cathedral in town. Jane says it is like a beautiful fairy castle. You eat ice-cream and swim in the public pool. Each night, you tell them stories about princesses and the moon.

This time you offer to drive us to the airport and I wonder if this means you are really doing better. Or are you faking all of this? You insist you are fine and I want to believe you. I can't stay here forever although I wish it were otherwise. We chat in the car and at the airport you get out and help me with my bags. Bending down on your haunches, you cuddle both girls and whisper softly in their ears the reminder that you love them more than the sun, the moon, the stars, and the sea. I search your eyes as you stand up. They look clear. You look clear. I squeeze you close and smell you. Your body is good to hold. You are still here. You confirm that you are not going anywhere in a hurry. I have to accept this and go home. I have already taken too much time off from the business and work is slipping. But how can I concentrate on anything else? I linger in your arms, holding you tightly before you shake me off mumbling, "Run along or you'll be late."

My arms struggle to drag the bags. I am tired. The girls seem happy enough to go home but I can't recall the last time I felt truly happy. Turning around one more time, I see your back as you climb into Ruth's car and drive out of sight. Inside the airport, I look at the people around me, but I can't distinguish anything. The world is murky. I board my flight and the whole human race dulls into the drone of the engine starting up; the engine of the plane that is about to fly me away, away from you. I fasten my seatbelt as I deliberate whether I should run to the pilot and stop the plane. I have made a mistake, I shouldn't be leaving. It isn't time. You aren't okay. I know you aren't okay.

32

I throw my unopened suitcase aside. Why am I home? I should turn around and go straight back to Cape Town. I shouldn't have left. The house smells of mildew from being closed up for ten days. As the girls run off to amuse themselves, I sit down at my desk and wonder how I'll ever be able to catch up with all the work. Flipping through unopened mail, I find a letter from the taxman reminding me that my extension for submitting the studio tax forms is the end of February. This means that I have two weeks left to work on this grueling assignment. I hang my head in weariness, and then freeze as I recognize your familiar handwriting on a different envelope. The letter. The one you mentioned. It hits me. I would have received this letter too late, had you had your way. I would have read it after you were dead. The girls are playing merrily in their room. I pour a cup of coffee, light a cigarette and sit down outside to read.

21 January 2007

Dearest Robyn

I write because I want to and because it's safer to sit here in this grim city bar and reel off thoughts to you, whom I trust, than try to engage with whatever this day is. It is as hot as a furnace – I am in my vest and boots, and could be mistaken for a beleaguered tramp (which isn't far off) and have walked to and from Greenpoint to listen to some jazz but found it unpleasant; the mix of good music with the comfortable sexualities in their telephones and g-strings. I look at them, their desire (and success) to be winners and wonder why I have such a problem with the entitled, those who feel that this world is rightfully theirs to inhabit. And then I think of Amanda and Barry, and see them there, too. Products of private schools trying to do their best. Maybe it was an early childhood of poverty, the harshness of an all-boy government school, the army that has made me fearful and loathsome of success. My now-rich parents who I feel never loved me enough.

I have just written a beautiful letter to a girl called Tammy, who is a waitress at Portabellos. I opened my Amazon-ordered Tom Waits parcel and she mentioned how long it had been since she got anything in the post. I took her address and said I would write to her, which I have. It will please her. But I am mad in the head; she reminds me so much of Amanda – her hands are the same, her lips similar, the caramel of her skin. The kind and funny things I wrote to her made me feel as though I am a betrayer, which is stupid, because there is nobody near me to betray.

I am in such a hole – a hole that I've always known existed and have, until now, managed to avoid. My nights are unbearable; I go to sleep shaking with tears and wake up the same way. I tell myself to try harder even though I am trying as hard as I can. I am completely at the end of my wits and know that, in the long run, a memory of me will be better for those I leave, than the existence of who I will become.

It's not just Amanda, my last love, but this whole physical

world; love is strangled by having to inhabit a body and those that can meld the two seem, to me, to be terrifying experiments into a realm that I want nothing to do with.

Despite what the entitled say, spirit and body are galaxies apart, and trying to make them one results in a grotesquerie that makes me ill to my stomach. I can't make them fit, I will choose to destroy one of them, and it won't be the spirit. But I am so afraid of leaving those who love me with so much pain and confusion and no matter how much I explain that I have not left, just removed the physical, I know that my words will not be understood; nobody believes the spirit is complete; they need the reality of ankles and eyes to complete their picture. And so, I must remain and keep those who love me intact in their illusions.

But should I find the strength and selfishness to be done with the physical, it will be up to you, dear Robyn, to have to explain to others what I will have done. A heavy call, it will stretch you further than you are capable of but I will be there, if you believe it, to help you. I will guide you through the girls' growth and guide them too. But leaving this world is not my immediate plan, I will decay as everyone does for the sake of my fragile friends, family, and lovers. I remember everything and sometimes think I can see the future and this is, perhaps, why I have such sleepless nights.

Fate is readable when love is pure, and if I am to either deny fate (or avoid seeing it), I need to find an impure love, the same garden variety that everyone else on this planet accepts. But I can't do this; having to carry my character, body, presence, and soul around is like an albatross around my spirit and to love someone on this planet would be like murdering them, such is my awareness of how things are.

And love, to me, is everything; it is the reason we exist – those who say the spirit is unique enough to exist without love are fools or in denial (keeping their fragile picture complete), and I know the reason that our spirits are as they are, is to love. At our ethereal essence, we are givers, not takers, but encumbered by the soul and physicality, reality, it is the other way around. I would rather be a giving spirit than a taking human, and, at the moment, I am neither. The twilight zone, perhaps; it could go either way.

Part of being on this planet is sex – not just part, but I believe it ruthlessly rules over the planet. Both men and women are obsessed with it, they measure themselves against themselves in terms of it. It is how people associate their essence, what they are capable of and what they have to avoid and confront. The physicality becomes spiritual; many people are afraid, more than I care to know have no borders because there is no substance to protect. I have become so tangled up in how I think of myself as a sexual creature on this planet, that I suspect I will never have sex again unless I pay for it...

I would rather be a giving spirit than a taking human, and so would Amanda; she is just stronger and more entitled than I and is unafraid to be selfish. I shudder to think what she and Barry get up to. I shudder to think what anyone gets up to. For this reason I hate mirrors – not the people type, who I find fascinating, but real ones, glass, paint...I am appalled by my face and body. How can I expect someone to love this? If I were an animal – a monkey, perhaps, in a troupe – I would be banished to the outer circle to pick up scraps and fornicate with the wounded and aged. But I am not an animal and even the wounded and aged are spared what I see in the mirror.

Amanda once said I should trust myself more. You've said as

much, echoing your guru's words; everyone says it – move on, take control, time will unfold, things change, be patient, go through doors not into walls… the list and advice is endless. These are the words from the fridge-world. No matter how sound their advice, it does not apply to me; I am different to them (despite what you might say – I know, I have spent a lifetime hiding myself, I know my secrets well) and my methods of keeping everything on 'normal' terms are wearing thin, I am losing steam and patience with being whom everyone wants to see, but the alternative is not pretty.

Again, I would rather be a giving spirit than a taking human.

I am tired, it is sweltering hot. I might go 'home', take a pill and sleep, and another when I wake, even though it's lunchtime all over the city.

Sorry for the heavy letter, the heavy life.

Love Stu

I get up and pace. I chain smoke. I read the letter again. There's a chill in the air but it's not the weather. I fret. How will I sleep? How will I be awake? What should I do? There is no break from my thoughts. I understand you. Yes, I always have. But you've gone over the edge. You wrote this letter one week before your attempt. One week. How can I trust you now?

33

Ruth calls to confirm that you are not looking well. She also tells me how you showed her your suicide note. The one we would have found if you hadn't been saved. It was in the accordion box. I remember the last message I received from you the day after your birthday, the day before your near-fatal swim in the dam. The message ended – 'The accordion in its case knows everything.' Ruth says that the suicide note said that you wanted to make sure that we all understood that no one was to blame, that this was your choice and that you hoped one day we would all understand.

Even though I am home, I haven't really left you. I carry you in my mind every waking moment and I toss and turn in the heat with terror all night. Your messages are still fraught. How long do I wait before I come back to Cape Town, try to hold you and tell you that this world is not such a bad place? How can I convince you to come home?

From: 'Stuart'
To: 'Robyn'
Sent: 09 February 2007 02:18 PM

Had a sleep/wake dream last night – I dreamt that the police came to take me away (to an asylum) and I didn't know who put them up to this and had to climb over the back wall and run – walked a million miles, made plans, mugged people for money, shaved, kept it tidy, lived under bridges – there was no one I could call, no one I could trust – not you, Amanda, Ruth, anyone; I couldn't risk asking for help. Exhausting.

Amanda phoned just now, nice to hear her voice; she said she wants to come down but I don't know – whether she wants to or feels she has to; and then she'll leave again... Phone calls, a Platonic friendship is good, but not enough. I want to see her, talk to her, hold her.

The whole newspaper is about sex this week, it seems – Valentine's Day coming and everyone plans their fucks, their frolics. Too depressing for words; I want to cut my cock off, or just the brain bit that makes it exist, along with love.

I miss Mr. Spooks.

From: 'Robyn'
To: 'Stuart'
Sent: 09 February 2007 08:55 PM

My darling Stuart, only a dream, I hope you know you can trust me, always and forever, I am on your side. I have been thinking so much about Mr. Spooks lately... wish he were with you now.

I got your letter, the one you kept asking me about. I have read it a few times, thank you for your thoughts. I want you to know that I understand and I love you. You will always be near to me.

You shouldn't be in the city. You are a country boy at heart. You need a house in the hills with jasmine and hedges and marbles hidden in shed roofs with German pointers sleeping on your veranda. There I see you madly scribbling away in your worn notebook, ideas for your next play, poem, composition, or characters in your novel. I see a large study and music room opening out onto greenery. Your whiskey glass sits next to your computer, which buzzes quietly waiting for you to enter all your genius into it. Grow your own herbs and vegetables. Play your accordion under the moon with only the crickets to hear you. Have the girls whenever you like. They love the country; they could be part of your life.

Quit your job, Stu. Get out of the city; make some money writing stories for various publications. Your nightmares will always be there, but your dreams will be sweeter. I will help you find this place. Anything is possible; I have told you this before. Maybe there will be a little pub nearby where you could play music. A simple life. Escape to your own thoughts, or madness, your own purity or depravity. Pack up, ship out, and find this place, this life, near your girls. xx

---

From: 'Stuart'
To: 'Robyn'
Sent: 10 February 2007 09:18 PM

have you been smoking the pots?

From: 'Stuart'
To: 'Robyn'
Sent: 11 February 2007 11:05 AM

my bike is fucked fucked – tried push starting it this morning to get out of town and must have snapped the drive shaft or something. I screamed and threw it down and eventually had to pay a tramp to help me push it up the hill.

I woke, as I went to bed, shattered with tears and loneliness and feel sick to my bones and everyone – you, Amanda, Ruth – is sick of me feeling sick to my bones and I need rescuing by Amanda, and her alone, who is fucking nowhere or fucking somewhere, doesn't love me enough, is a million miles away eating or washing dishes or screwing with her mouth open or playing with her children or driving or whatever and all I think about is her and how she isn't near me and is near someone else.

I am at work although it isn't a work day and that's fucked up. Will go to buy envelopes and butter and then, against all good advice inside myself, get fucked at the pub so that I might sleep this afternoon and when I wake up will get fucked again so I can sleep tonight. In between I will make every drunken effort not to call Amanda, as she's said I must whenever I want because I won't know what to say and Barry will be eyeballing her out.

I want to break something, preferably myself.

From: 'Robyn'
To: 'Stuart'
Sent: 11 February 2007 08:16 PM

Stu, I am so sorry. I wish there was something I could do to help. I want to say just come home! I know you think it's not an option for you, but I want you to know that it is an option. Or think about living close to Durban in the country as I suggested before when you thought I was on pot!

This is a time for serious considerations about things… work, money, and everything else is not important AT all. Remember when you left your job, to write your book and we said we'd be okay. Well it'll be the same now. Just think about perhaps making some changes, even if they are just temporary.

Some reasons I wish you were closer are selfish too, other than for the girls, I am struggling. I feel like the house is falling apart and I can't do everything on my own. Feeding pets and kids is about all I can manage. But it'll be okay; I know you won't come back. I just hate you being all alone there when you could just be here which would be better for all of us. No expectations. How can I help?

From: 'Stuart'
To: 'Robyn'
Sent: 12 February 2007 10:11 AM

If you want to help, can you get me some industrial-strength sleeping tablets from your doctor? I can't fuck up again.

34

It was only five days ago that I was loathe to leave you in Cape Town. I try to remember every word, every fleeting look. To persuade myself that I will see you again. Food remains half eaten; dishes pile up on the sink. Admin overflows on my desk. I can't focus. I should never have left you. You need me. I pace... I smoke... I worry. There must be more I can do. I felt helpless when I read your message asking for sleeping tablets. I knew it. I knew you hadn't ditched your plan of dying. I can't be part of that plan. How much time do I have? I don't know how to save a life. Who can help me? How can I help you leave this dark place? You used to be so passionate, so full of life. Then you spiraled downward. Now you are dropping, free falling. Can I catch you? Do you want me too? I picture you as seven years old again. You're falling. I run after you, trying to help; to stop you from hurting yourself. What else can I do? There must be something.

I pick up the phone and dial Amanda's number. She answers. I explain that the situation is extremely serious and ask if there is any way she could fly down to see you for a day, to buy me some time until I can think of something else. There is no time for thought, no time for delay. Can she go tomorrow? Please. She sounds upset and says that she doesn't know if this is what is best for you. She wants to talk to a psychologist to seek guidance. At this stage, I'm concerned about keeping you here day by day. Amanda says she'll call me later. She never does.

I call Ruth. She tells me that you are looking awful and she will stay with you tonight. I breathe a small sigh of relief. Between Ruth and me, we are trying our best. You must hate this, the two of us fussing over you so. Watching you. Waiting. I'm sure you want to be left alone, but we just can't do that.

You need saving. I am the incessant savior. Since I was a young girl I've rescued. I used to bring home stray pets, searching them out in every possible place. I still do this. I have a house full of pets and among them the deaf, the blind, the one-eyed. It's become a joke among my friends who refer to me affectionately as Saint Francis. After school I studied to become a missionary, planning to go and teach children in Central Africa. To save them. Ruth is a rescuer too. But even the two of us together can't save you from yourself now.

From: 'Stuart'
To: 'Robyn'
Sent: 12 February 2007 02:57 PM

Am off tomorrow. had such a fraught night last night...
climbing walls with aloneness, phoned Amanda, she had to
explain to Barry who she was speaking to and I just thought
that I am nothing more than a nuisance and put the phone
down on her... she called Ruth at 2 a.m. worried about me. I
miss her so. I need her arms around me. I mustn't bother her.
Or anyone else.

I posted poems onto Gumtree Freebies site in London.

I light another cigarette and look up your poems on Gumtree
London. I identify them immediately. You have called yourself
Norbert, Amanda's nickname for you, and have used a different
e-mail address. An idea begins to form in my mind. I hardly
think about it before it's already happening. If I can't reach you,
perhaps somebody else can. Someone new. I can create this
someone, and you may even like her. She will message you in
response to your poem and just maybe, a stranger from the other
side of the world will be able to reach you. You can
communicate with her and tell her everything that you think we
are all so tired of hearing. It is perfect. I have found another way
to try and save you.

I open a remote yahoo.uk account. I choose a random name,
Leila, Leila Summers. A picture of her forms in my mind's eye.
She is 35 years old. Single. Fair-skinned with brown eyes and
long mousy brown hair. She is small and slight and wears
librarian glasses that slip down her freckled nose. She is shy and
introverted. Her ginger cat is named Francis and is her only

companion. Leila loves reading poetry and rich literature. She lives in an upstairs apartment in West Sussex, London and doesn't go out much. She eats at the Italian restaurant a block away every day for lunch. Most days she visits the secondhand corner bookshop on her way home where she spends hours reading or writing and drinking cappuccino. She is lonely and disillusioned with love. She drinks whiskey, bites her nails, and suffers terribly from insomnia.

If Leila can get under your skin, you will have a new confidant. Maybe she will need you more than you need her and you can have an opportunity to play the role of savior, which you also do well whenever it is required. Leila needs to stand out, above all the other responses you receive. She has the upper hand – I know you better than most.

First, a quote from Jean-Paul Sartre. I cross my fingers as Leila sends you a message. From my deepest being – I pray or something damn close – that this will work. All I am hoping for is another chance.

From: 'Leila Summers'
To: 'Norbert'
Sent: 12 February 2007 04:26 PM

Dear Norbert

Your poem is beautiful. Would you send me more?

Leila
<attached - quote from Jean-Paul Sartre>

I wait. I think about Leila. I smoke. I check messages. How will she hold your attention? Flattery? Weakness? Similarity? You must respond. I check again, and there it is!

From: 'Norbert'
To: 'Leila Summers'
Sent: 12 February 2007 05:47 PM

Dear Leila – how can I refuse? Sartre, kind words...

I send warm regards from Cape Town on the other side of our little and vast planet.

Stuart
What sort of a name is Norbert anyway..!!!?)
<attached - poems>

You send Leila all your poems. I take time to formulate an answer. I have to be clever about this. This is not a game. This is my final chance. Leila can't be one of the crowd. She needs to be *the one*.

I chew my pen and have another cigarette. I know how much you desire praise; how you long for it in the depth of your being. Although it looks different to the outside world, I know how small you see yourself, how worthless and insignificant. Leila will flatter you and then grab your attention by touching on subjects close to your heart. She can't sound anything like me; I will have to be careful. You know me too well. I go to sleep with the first bit of hope I've felt in a long time.

The next day I arrive at Susie's for my appointment and let her in on my plan. She likes it and offers to help. We throw around some ideas. I rush home and message a close friend of mine who has moved to London and share the plan with her. She is shocked but hugely supportive. She gives me details of West Sussex and agrees to let me use her postal address.

And so Leila becomes real. She lives in a real town and has a physical address. She loves to read, usually the same books as you. She loves philosophy. But there is weakness, too. She has been disappointed by the world. She needs a friend.

From: 'Leila Summers'
To: 'Norbert'
Sent: 13 February 2007 12.42 AM

Dear Stuart!

Many thanks. I spent the evening reading your poems. It's cold and gloomy here and they warmed me.

Leila

From: 'Leila Summers'
To: 'Norbert'
Sent: 13 February 2007 09:01 PM

Dear Stuart

I have to say that your poems are brilliant. Who is the sentimental man behind these amazing words? Who are you, Stuart? I am curious to know. Your writing is exquisite; your words have such powerful feeling yet curious meaning. Inspire me some more.

Leila
<attached – poem by Edgar Allan Poe>

I spend hours at night reading and researching your favorite authors. I scan the books you've been telling me to read for nearly a decade. I read your favorite poets. I've never done this before. Leila messages you every day. You like her. You talk to Ruth about her. You open up to her. Maybe Leila can save you.

35

The most insignificant thing about today is that it is Valentine's Day. As I sit down at my computer with my first cup of coffee of the day, Leila and I check messages. There is a Valentine's Day story from you, for both of us. You also ask me to drop off a copy with Amanda.

From: 'Stuart'
To: 'Leila Summers'
Sent: 14 February 2007 09:52 AM

Hello

Here is the saddest Valentine's Day story in the world that I wrote last night for nobody and everybody in particular. Should you want to let me have a postal address, I will gladly post you some of my music from here in Cape Town. Google may tell you a wee bit more about me. Your kind words are received gratefully; I have had some such funny and lovely responses from my spoofy Gumtree advert. My day at work begins, I am tired from insomnia and a noisy neighborhood (The Bo Kaap, colorful, traditional, rowdy). Will you try to read Nicole Krauss's "The History of Love"? I finished this yesterday; a formidable book...

Stuart

The Garden of Love

I sit quietly now, in the heady silence of an early evening, filled with beauty and sadness – beauty because it is so lovely here, sadness because this place has seen so much love.

It is where I have lived for many years, alone, except for the early evenings, such as now, when they would come and I would undress them, kiss them on their lips and send them off to their loves. But this evening there is nobody here. Perhaps there are no more left. Perhaps those remaining are wrapped in the arms of love, preparing meals with love, sighing softly after love. Perhaps I am the last one to be sent off to my love, but I know there will be others coming, the next generation, there will always be others. And they will need me and I will undress them, as I have done to so many, kiss them on their lips, both men and women, and send them off to their loves.

From where I sit, on this wide smooth rock, polished by so many bare feet, I look down the flow of water to where it fills into the deep pond way below. In the dimming light, I can still see how clear it is, how warm and forgiving. The familiar and tireless gurgle as the falling water becomes one with the pond sounds no less different this evening than it does when they are here. Why should it? I have made it so, it knows not to tire or change, it is constant, it will flow for as long as water exists, as long as love exists, as long as I exist.

Many seasons ago I came here. I discovered it by accident while walking my thoughts away. It was beautiful even then, but without the beauty of human love that is more beautiful than anything the Earth can offer. I stood at the top of this waterfall and could smell the sea a little way away, behind the dense foliage of the trees that have kept this place hidden from everyone who has love. The pond below was as clear as it is now but cluttered with branches and leaves from the Frangipani trees that encircle it. That night, I stayed here and have not left since. I took off my clothes and sat on this rock until the moon was replaced with the sun and then I slept, curled upon the rock, my arms around my knees, the sound of falling water stilling my heart. It has never been cold and I have never worn clothing again.

The next day I began to clear the branches, leaves, and Frangipani flowers from the pond. I trimmed back overhanging foliage and moved rocks around in symbols of love: circles for tenderness, cairns for strength, pebbles for humor and affection, solitary boulders for passion. In between these I shaped the soil, loosened it with my fingers and replanted wild flowers that grew in the shade nearby on the beach. And at the water's edge and beneath the waterfall, I planted ferns with leaves small and strong like rows of green piano keys. They glistened in the fine mist the falls made in the evenings when they used to come. Above the falls, I traced the stream up the rocky gully until I found its source. It gushed and sparkled from between two huge rocks, from inside the Earth, and had a purity of un-tampered minerals to it when brought to the tongue. Over the many years I have been here, it has never swollen with the rain, dwindled in drought or altered in its compound. It is constant and pure, much like love itself. Then I began to nurse the pond. Using logs, I levered great rocks and the stump of a fallen tree into place that would enable me to drain the top few meters of the pond into the sea further below. This took me many moons and during this time, the first one arrived. She undressed and helped me construct the wooden mechanism that would allow the stump to open the pond down into the ocean. And then we maneuvered rocks against the sheer face above the pond and made a curling staircase to the top. In between the steps we planted small delicate ferns and draped flowering vines over the railing we made out of polished driftwood. Around the rock at the top we built a balcony out of yellowwood with a little gate overlooking the fall and carved names into the uprights with a sharp shell I found on the beach.

At night, she slept on the rock at the top of the falls, where I am sitting now, the balcony, her arms wrapped around her knees. I slept in a cove behind the falls on a mattress of Frangipani flowers I gathered in the late afternoons, just above the pond. On some nights, when there was a moon out, I could look through the falling water and see a hundred faces, each more beautiful than the next, each one as pure as the other. While she stayed with me, in the small hours, the woman above on the rock used to sing softly to herself in her sleep.

There is a hardy and beautiful plant that grows near the water's edge. It has millions of tiny white flowers like stars and swollen leaves that smell faintly of mint. When these flowers are eaten, half a handful, the heart goes into a reverie and the mind forgets and sleeps and everything is stripped away until love stands naked and warm, unmovable in the very soul. I tend this plant with much care and have not eaten any of its flowers since the day I first discovered it, many seasons ago.

The woman stayed for six moons and on the sixth, she ate the flowers, I kissed her on her lips and she unhooked the balcony railing, stepped off and fell asleep in the pond below. Using the lever we had built, I opened the pond and she went out to sea. I replaced the stump and the pond refilled itself before she and her love became one with the waves. On the balcony, she had carved "Lex."

Soon after, a man came. He was old, very old and walked with difficulty. I undressed him, gave him the flowers that look like stars, helped him climb the rock staircase, handed him the shell, and he carved a name; I kissed his lips and refilled the pond. "Dawn."

The next afternoon, another man came with a woman. They sat for a long time next to the pond holding each other's hands. When they stood, I undressed them, gave them flowers, kissed their lips, they kissed each other once, very feelingly, climbed the stairs, and I refilled the pond. They had each carved "You" into the balcony in the same place so that it looked like there was just one word.

And then they came. Every afternoon. Men, women, boys, girls, the old and the young, the attractive, the ugly. I kissed hundreds of soft lips and refilled the pond. At night, behind the water, on my mattress of flowers, I heard each and every one of them singing in their sleep. Gentle love songs of joy, peace and beauty underscored by the steady gurgle of falling water. It is what I hear now, sitting on the rock, the balcony. It is what I will hear when I turn to my mattress of flowers in a short while to get some rest. Because, even though they have stopped coming, I know there will be more. They will come as soon as love shifts her seasons again.

It takes me hours to compose a poem from Leila in response to your Garden of Love story. I haven't written poetry for years and worry about knowing how judgmental you are of other people's writing. As I press send, I clench my teeth.

From: 'Leila Summers'
To: 'Stuart'
Sent: 14 February 2007 11.53 PM

Dear Stuart

Your story was haunting and beautifully melancholic. Forgive my past forwardness. I would feel fortunate to receive your music: <address>

I have not read Nicole Krauss but will look out for her. Thank you for the recommendation.

I hesitantly send you this in response to your "saddest Valentine's Day story in the world."

I carry a kiss upon pallid brow
The burnished rock cradles me now
Letters of the name I will not carve
Covenant sealed with blossoms like stars
Low full moon lights the vortex below
Memories whelm from a lifetime ago
Whispering rhythms of love's own quest
Transient beauty calls me to rest
Gentle ballads fill my dreams
Of colors that have been or could be
Slender fingers of silver foam prey
White horses bear me away

36

In between struggling to compose the poem, spending time with the girls and tidying the house, I receive another unsettling message from you.

From: 'Stuart'
To: 'Robyn'
Sent: 14 February 2007 04:35 PM

The more and the clearer I think about things, the more I realize I shouldn't be here. I have sent the four adults in my life — you, Amanda, Ruth & Beverley — into therapy and know that I cannot live without Amanda. The more we have been talking recently, the more I know she will not be with me, the more I know I will not be with anyone else. And life is almost over and I don't want to live it out in loneliness like Pete or survival like everyone else.

On Valentine's night, while couples around the city are wining and dining and sharing love, I meet with a friend who has invited an experienced psychiatric nurse to join us for a look at my options to help you. I disclose everything and she listens carefully before sharing some insights with me from her twenty-plus years experience in the field. She suspects that you may suffer from bipolar type 2 disorder, and explains how a person with this disorder could live a relatively normal life until they encounter a significant trigger. This could be any number of things, different for each individual. Once this trigger is set off, the person can spin into a negative downward spiral which can then only be stopped by medication. The alternative is often suicide.

I nod in understanding and swallow a large mouthful of wine. I have already done substantial research on this disorder. Your trigger was not necessarily Amanda herself, but perhaps the powerful feelings she unleashed in you. The nurse tries to convince me that the only way to save you is to have you locked away against your will and medicated. In South Africa, the procedure would require me to file an affidavit in which I claim that you are a danger to yourself. A police officer would then arrest and handcuff you and take you to a general state hospital where you will be held for a maximum of seventy-two hours for examination. During this time, you will undergo an initial psychiatric assessment. Involuntary admission needs to be justified on the basis that the person is mentally ill and constitutes a threat to themselves or others. I would have to be present to fill in the forms.

While I am listening I already predict that you will easily be able to convince the doctors otherwise. You certainly don't come across as being unstable in public and would do anything in your power to avoid going to hospital. In the highly unlikely event that the evaluation indicates a need for involuntary mental health care intervention, a review board will authorize your admission to a state psychiatric facility for up to thirty days, although she informs me that, in her experience, they won't keep you for longer than two weeks. While there, you will receive the appropriate treatments which may include sedation, forced medication, mechanical restraint if necessary, psychiatric counseling, and possible electro-convulsive therapy. They will then release you and advise continuation of your treatment as an outpatient. I find myself laughing out loud. As if! I ask her if there is any way that I can make sure you would be detained for longer than two weeks. She admits that it is unlikely. She describes Valkenberg Psychiatric Hospital in Cape Town as an overcrowded institution in a wretched state with most of the patients being criminals under psychiatric observation. Still, she highly recommends I follow this option even though it isn't going to be easy. The alternative, she says, is unthinkable.

I sit and sip on my wine, not wanting to seem ungrateful or let on that I would never be able to go this route. It doesn't make sense to me. Although I obviously agree that you are a threat to yourself, I doubt very much whether it would even get to the point where you would be admitted involuntarily. You are just too smart for that. And even if by some remote chance you were admitted, I just don't see how locking you up would be a solution. After two weeks of being force medicated, you would never continue medication or treatment. I also know that even if one has a mental illness, finding the correct medication and dosage takes a lot longer than two weeks. Aside from medication, what you need is ongoing therapy which you have already refused. The whole thing doesn't seem viable to me. The only pro is that you will be kept alive for an additional two weeks but during that time you will have lost the last few people who you trust. You will die entirely alone.

I come home and research depression and bipolar type 2 disorder again. The symptoms and characteristics of this disorder do not describe you accurately. I am still not convinced that you have an illness of the brain. You are unquestionably depressed but it seems to me that your mind and heart are sick and for this, you need determination, therapy, and a will to live. The body, which you want to destroy, has done you no wrong. It is your mind that is needy, black, and miserable. You used to joke about being a lunatic; claiming to be influenced into wild foolishness and abandonment by the phases of the moon. Buddha says that all suffering, pain, sorrow, and mental anguish are caused by the mind and that lunatics are people with no control over their minds. It goes completely against nature to want to harm one's body but if the mind was sick, one could consider this extreme to escape the pain. The alternative to destroying the body would be to conquer the mind. If your mind view can be altered this would certainly provide some relief and you could perhaps move towards happiness and taking control of your life. As I see it, therapy and a personal journey into healing the mind or soul would be first prize. Either way, I'm not sure that it matters what I or anybody else thinks because I know you won't buy any of it.

The one thing I know for sure on this Valentine's Day is that I love you. So I e-mail you to remind you of this again. I cannot allow you to die without knowing how much you are loved.

37

From: 'Stuart'
To: 'Robyn'
Sent: 15 February 2007 09:40 AM

I tried to explain to Ruth last night that what I want is not destructive, the opposite. She freaked out and is having a nervous breakdown. I need you, Amanda and Ruth not to criticize my wishes but to understand. It is too hard for you all, it will take much time. x

I allow the quiet strokes of my pencil and compass to guide me. I am drawing an angel. This is my third Mandala painting workshop with Gita. The classes are relaxing and therapeutic and in the past they took me away from the madness for an hour or two. But this morning I am restless and can't settle down. The table vibrates and my cell phone lights up. Each time this happens a panic grips me and I am filled with the too-familiar fear that this call will be the one I dread. The message is from Ruth and reads – 'He is still planning to fucking do it!'

I take my phone and cigarettes outside and call Ruth right back. She is hiding in the bathroom at work. Through jagged sobs, she chokes out that you are quite clear you are still going to kill yourself and that she can't cope anymore. Your parents are also sick with worry. This morning your mom phoned Amanda to ask her to leave you alone. Ruth and I briefly discuss the possibility of involuntary admission. Instead, I propose coming down to Cape Town again to give her some relief.

My hands are shaking so fiercely that I can barely pick up the paint brush. Tears fall and mix with the paint. I cry an ocean that washes onto the page and, as I persevere through blurry eyes, the painting becomes a blue and green angel. I tell the angel, my angel, that I need him now.

From: 'Stuart'
To: 'Robyn'
Sent: 15 February 2007 01:20 PM

Apparently, Ruth said, mom phoned Amanda. Oh boy.

You don't have to and I don't expect you to, don't really expect anyone to understand – not even you, my friend – but if you can ask your doc for some pills, I would be grateful.

I book an air ticket to come to Cape Town in two days' time. The girls will have to go and stay with your parents for a long weekend; I need to see you alone. I ring you at work and plead that you stop talking about killing yourself immediately. Everyone is distraught with worry. It is too much to bear. Just stop. No one can be expected to understand. It's beyond human capability. Please. I let you know I'll be there in two days' time and I want you to still be there. You agree.

Then I call Amanda. She is still upset after speaking to your mom. I suggest to her that if she has anything she needs to say to you, she might want to write it in a letter for me to give you. I point out that this could be her last opportunity. She says I mustn't talk that way. She doesn't give me anything.

From: 'Stuart'
To: 'Robyn'
Sent: 15 February 2007 04:36 PM

You know – you don't have to come down; I won't do anything rash, Ruth's okay, I'm okay – forget pills and trauma, I'll be fine.

Hope you haven't had to field a hundred fraught phone calls. xx

---

From: 'Stuart'
To: 'Leila Summers'
Sent: 15 February 2007 05:06 PM

<attached – short story & photograph>

From: 'Leila Summers'
To: 'Stuart'
Sent: 15 February 2007 06:01 PM

Stuart

You keep surprising me. I am overwhelmed by your writing. I want to know more. Google does not begin to explain someone who could express these feelings. The smoky picture interests me.

Leila

From: 'Stuart'
To: 'Leila Summers'
Sent: 16 February 2007 09:40 AM

Helloo

This morning, on the way to work, I posted you a CD of music. It makes me feel peculiarly pleased to post songs to someone on the other side of the globe that I don't know. Just because I can. Have a good weekend!

Stu
<attachment – poems>

From: 'Leila Summers'
To: 'Stuart'
Sent: 16 February 2007 03:34PM

I look forward to receiving your CD and listening to your music. If it is anything like your writing, I know I will be impressed. I am grateful for more poems. I feel slightly embarrassed at having sent you my amateurish attempt the other night and take your silence on the subject as a kindness. I choose rather to send you pieces that I have enjoyed as below.

Leila
<attachment – quote from Gabriel Garcia Marquez>

From: 'Stuart'
To: 'Leila Summers'
Sent: 16 February 2007 04:50 PM

Marquez... ah! What can I say? Forgive me my silence on

your poem – not 'a kindness'! It made me uneasy – perhaps just the heavy subject matter and a direct related response, words and visions, makes me back off. I was in a coma two weeks ago after being hauled out of the bottom of a lake and a hundred sleeping pills. A long time coming and still open-ended. The garden of love. I didn't know how to respond, what you could see or imagine, but thank you!

Would you like to read some hard erotica? Not to be taken with literary merit but solely designed to make a reader wet and warm. Writing has no borders, realities can be invented and realities come in all shapes and sizes. But you may find them offensive – you may be twelve years old! Or eighty!

I am tired of my work day; a couple of hours left, my veranda calls. Google Image Bo-Kaap in Cape Town to see the colorful suburb I stay in.

I attach a couple of pics of my veranda where I while away sleepless hours every night. And another bad story.

Stuart

From: 'Leila Summers'
To: 'Stuart'
Sent: 16 February 2007 11:26 PM

Stuart

I wish to pass up the offer of hard erotica for the moment. Lust can eclipse passion and love. There is enough disillusionment on these issues. I enjoy the writings you send me. I am not twelve or eighty but just about somewhere directly in between. I hope I do not disappoint you.

I am somewhat confused. Your words and feelings of love

seem so deep yet you have said you tried to take your life? If you don't mind me asking, what!? could bring a man such as yourself who is filled with such beauty to that point? The tiny glimpse of you I see doesn't fit the picture that you paint. I know this may be too personal to ask, but seeing as you brought it up.

Bo-Kaap looks like a wonderful place and insomnia sounds too familiar.

Leila

A friend pays for a phone session for me with a psychic. She has updated the psychic with my situation. This makes me wary but I go ahead and make the call anyway. The first thing the woman assures me is that she can see five guides around me at that moment and that I must need a lot of help. Hah! If she only knew! She goes on to say that your mind is disconnected and tormented. You have rational moments but are in a constant state of trauma. Your soul levels, she adds, are perfectly in balance. You are walking along a thin edge of a knife. You could go either way. She suggests I go to you without judgment, leaving any expectations or needs behind. She explains that this is a time of healing; a sacred time. This is about my journey. I need to act in integrity and surrender as it is not in my hands. She reminds me that all death is a choice on a soul level; whether we choose to go by car accident, heart attack, or suicide, it's all our decision. Although I am skeptical and not entirely sure that I believe any of this, I feel much more peaceful after the consultation. I am ready to come and see you tomorrow.

38

It's a sunny Saturday morning as the airplane rushes onto the runway in Cape Town. Walking the familiar tarmac, I have a peculiar sense of five body-guards walking behind me wearing suits and dark glasses. Their presence is so compelling that I turn around and I have to laugh at myself for doing so. Bradley gives me a lift into the city. I have the day to myself until you and Ruth finish your weekend shift at eleven p.m. The shops down Long Street keep me busy for a number of hours. The cosmopolitan street with its fascinating clash of cultures is lined with bars and restaurants, secondhand stores and other alluring nooks and crannies. In the late afternoon when I'm worn out from walking, I immerse myself as Leila at the Internet cafe. In between messaging you at work, I head outside for cigarettes, and then later dinner at a trendy hamburger joint. I am the only one there who is eating alone.

From: 'Stuart'
To: 'Leila Summers'
Sent: 17 February 2007 12:51 PM

Hello

Of course – thank you for not making me a depravity monger; my realities are so tangled, your words elicit respect and bring needed balance.

Love and beauty is everything to me, the reason we are alive – I feel so utterly un-entitled to this. A life without love is half a life and half a life does not invite love. My love is in Durban, 2,000km away, with her family, where she belongs. I have never known such un-vaulting love before, will never know such love again; my every waking moment, my sleepless nights, are filled with awe and bewilderment and I sometimes feel that I will pass out from pining and unrequite. As does she.

Despite what the history of the heart and poems say, survival is bigger than our dreams and I know that my dreams are the only place I understand – sometimes. I have inspired madness and unbearable anxiety to the three people I care about trying to explain that death by choice is not destructive, that it can be a placed thing, a portal to peace for the departed and remaining. Needless to say, nobody will or can understand. And so I let it rest, am silent on this and should not have brought it up with you, either. Perhaps it is a stranger's task to hear unplaced aches that those at hand should not...

But it's not all doom and gloom. I sat this morning at a cafe in Long Street and watched the passers-by and forced my selfish heart to adore them, to smile upon the gentle sways of lovers, the tottering of the infirm, the insectile scrambling of children, the slope of the sly, the weight of the poor, the swagger of the entitled. It was an effort and I eventually fell to breathing in the day around them because it is bright and blue today with high scudding clouds and I felt foolish for all the thoughts that had me pacing last night. And now I eat an apple and look forward to waging war on words of the world until 11 p.m. tonight at work.

There was a story yesterday which said that research has

shown that those madly in love show the same chemical symptoms as a cocaine addict. Maybe being a cocaine addict would be better; at least it can be cured.

It's funny that I write to you, from out of nowhere. It makes me glad. Whether you are 12 or 80 is irrelevant; your words sound kind, sad and are pleasant to receive.

I send kind thoughts.

Stuart
<attachment – a poem>

Try to see a film "Gloomy Sunday".

From: 'Leila Summers'
To: 'Stuart'
Sent: 17 February 2007 04:05 PM

Stuart

I have often asked myself if unrequited love is not better than never having truly experienced love and beauty at all. But I still don't find an answer. Reality is confusing. I ponder this.

You say a life without love is half a life and love and beauty are the reason we are alive. And you have found this love and she has found you. Is the need for real hands and lips greater than the need for real love? Will your portal of peace bring you these hands and lips? And why is it that you feel that being madly in love is something that should be cured?

If I speak of things I do not understand, forgive me.

Leila

From: 'Stuart'
To: 'Leila Summers'
Sent: 17 February 2007 04:33 PM

Dear Leila

It sounds as if you understand these things better than I. I wish I had the strength of character to accept that I was, am loved, that my love is accepted. You are right; reality is confusing. Is waking up with someone you love sleeping alongside you confusing? Is waking up alone with a head full of visions and dreams less confusing? I would give anything to wake up with her. But then, reality – it's more than just soft mornings, isn't it? I am so flummoxed. I have such a sex heart, too – desire can be consuming, it frightens me sometimes. I know this to be an essential part of real love, within the spiritual, closeness confirmed; we are a fearful species. Perhaps the peace that I seek is the peace of nothingness. But I will be placed; careful, selfless. I am loved, I must be more... Buddhist?... about this.

I sense a melancholy in you, Leila, my new faraway mysterious friend – despite my flailings and garbled confessions, there is beauty, there is grace. I hope you will be able to find and feel this in between my fraught words.

Thank you for your thoughts.

Stuart

From: 'Stuart'
To: 'Leila Summers'
Sent: 17 February 2007 05:47 PM

Jealousy is a killer.

From: 'Leila Summers'
To: 'Stuart'
Sent: 17 February 2007 08:48 PM

You are wrong, Stuart, I do not think I understand these things at all. I question only because I long to understand. Waking up softly with someone sounds wondrous, but it makes me sad to think about. In my experience, it falls a long way from dreams. Perhaps dreams are not such a bad place to dwell. Reality can be cold and must be obliged. I don't know what else I think. Perhaps the daffodils will inspire me tomorrow.

Leila

From: 'Leila Summers'
To: 'Stuart'
Sent: 17 February 2007 09:11 PM

Interesting. I wonder then, should one just expect the same uppers and downers? And could one then substitute the word love instead of cocaine in articles such as this:

"With continued use, many cocaine addicts develop a higher tolerance for the drug over time. Addicts are also said to 'chase the high'; meaning they continue to use cocaine seeking the feeling they felt the first time they used it. For people addicted to cocaine and cocaine effects, this high will never again be felt in the same way, and this addiction can lead to insanity and death."

From: 'Stuart'
To: 'Leila Summers'
Sent: 17 February 2007 09:31 PM

Good Lord. Please tell me that this is a malaise of coke heads alone... I am fiddling with a song that goes something like: Love is pure... when it's down.

Maybe we should go and live in a zoo. Commit ourselves completely to an elephant or a gnu and have a deep meaningful relationship that is warts and all companionable. Scratch my back, I'll scratch yours, &c. Be kind to each other, accept table and toilet manners...

Have you read Paulo Coelho's "Eleven Minutes"? He irritates me a bit but it is stirring.

Stuart

From: 'Stuart'
To: 'Leila Summers'
Sent: 17 February 2007 09:41 PM

I had a dog once – a German Pointer (who was missing his one front leg and his tail – the breeders would be horrified!) called Mr. Spooks. He was my dearest friend. He grew old, arthritis crept in. When I think of him, I smile; his gummy jowls, his befuddled eyes, his woozy snore. I don't think of him sadly or achingly, I am grateful I knew him, we did so much stuff together, we were mates, slept in the same bed... Perhaps love can be considered such; without being greedy – us in our mid-lives have surely known love, perhaps we can learn to smile back on love instead of keening towards it.

A bit of a bleak outlook, perhaps, but (as I tell myself all the time) baby steps as we approach an unknown future: we don't know what's around the corner, at the next bus stop, under a near umbrella! Maybe your daffodils are a guide in disguise...

I have two girls - Jane, 6, and Rose, 4. They are in Durban with their mother, who is a dear friend. This love – child love – is a heartening lesson, in loving selflessly without touch, physicality, needs. I try to draw from this. But it doesn't make stuff go away.

Another hour and a half of work left. Leila – however you take this; I send you love. Your words are edited and quiet, you seem embattled somehow. But I know you respect and feel love and maybe, from 14,000 miles away, if I send out a warm thought into the Cape Town air, you might pick it up amongst your daffodils. Will you try? Over the next hour or so, it will be waiting for you there!

Take care, back at work on Monday.

Stuart
<attached – picture of daffodils>

From: 'Leila Summers'
To: 'Stuart'
Sent: 17 February 2007 09:48 PM

Stuart

Thank you for the unexpected friendship from a stranger on the other side of the world. Tomorrow, I will try and pick some daffodils, the weather has been fine and they have just arrived. Goodnight, until Monday then.

Leila

At ten o'clock I walk back down Long Street where I wait for you and Ruth at the arranged meeting place, a bar. When you arrive together, we drink and make small talk and Ruth and I act as if we don't notice your somber mood. It is understood that I take over the suicide watch now for four days.

You and I walk up the cobbled Bo Kaap streets in silence to your house. Sitting in our usual spot on the gray chairs, you proceed to tell me about a new e-mail friendship you have with a girl in England named Leila. I have to maintain a dead-pan face as you comment on how pleasant it is to be able to communicate with her. I slurp a twinge of jealousy back with my coffee and remind myself ridiculously that *I am* Leila.

39

I wake up late and wander into the kitchen, heading straight for the kettle. In the sunny courtyard outside the back of your house is a long wooden bench where I find you smoking a cigarette and plucking on the guitar. A white envelope on the kitchen counter captures my attention as I recognize your mom's handwriting. She had phoned me two weeks back to seek advice on what to write to you in a letter. I indicated then that the only need was to let you know that she loves you. While stirring my coffee, I eye the letter and, noticing, you point out that I am welcome to read it. The card contains a brief note of general family news which ends abruptly with the words – 'much love, Mom.' I slide it back into the envelope and sneak a quick look at you.

"Stuart... you do understand that your mom and dad love you very much, don't you?" I state as nonchalantly as I can. You give me an upward nod and take a measured drag from your cigarette as I persist, "Well, um, sometimes maybe they just don't know how to show it."

You keep tinkering away on the guitar strings with flat fingers and nails bitten to the quick; an indication of your nervousness with yourself and the world. I subtly wipe away a tear as you look sideways at me in disgust. I picture you again as a grubby seven-year-old boy in baggy shorts and a hand-me-down shirt; stubborn and committed, even then. I want to dart outside, throw down that old guitar and grab you in my arms as if you are that young child. But you are a grown man now capable of making your own decisions. So I drink my coffee and stare at you as if I need to memorize every feature; the stubborn chin, the soft lines, the curves, the furrow of your brow. When I join you outdoors, you slide uncomfortably away and lay down your guitar. We smoke in silence until I have an idea. I suggest a foot massage, which I know you won't turn down.

For the past year, your feet have been plagued by athlete's foot. On the last trip I told you that, according to my Louise Hay book, this means *frustration at not being accepted and an inability to move forward*. To which you sneered and said it was something you caught in a shower. We listen to a haunting piece of classical music. For over an hour I rub every inch of your small, scaly feet with the tea tree oil that Amanda sent you when you came out of the hospital. These feet have rubbed themselves together for all the time I have known you as a subconscious way of comforting yourself to sleep; a habit that had once irritated me but which I grew to love. I massage with tenderness, working slowly and gently, endeavoring to put happy thoughts into every stroke so that they might soak in with the oil. You're on my watch, and I am well aware that it may be my last.

Afterwards, we take a Sunday stroll. Your motorbike has broken down again and stands lifeless on the pavement in front of your house. The rest of the world fades away as we walk, heading nowhere in particular. Now and then we hold hands. At times I watch you from behind as you stride on ahead. Your feet touch the ground with a familiar unevenness. And for this moment I am just glad to see you walking, still here on this earth.

We saunter through the city and across a park where you stop to collect acorns for the girls. Carefully selecting the finest ones, you put them into your pocket and keep going. I carry mine in my hand. They are smooth and warm as I roll them around in my palm. They are perfect; the way I see your essence. There is no dialogue. It seems an effort enough for you to continue to put one foot in front of the other, moving forward step by step.

I think back to a weekend we spent in a stone cave in the mountains with Mr. Spooks when Jane was only six months old. Mr. Spooks was getting older and suffered from arthritis in his one and only front leg. We had gone for a walk and Mr. Spooks wasn't able to keep up. You picked him up, slung him over your shoulders and sang – 'He's not heavy, he's my brother.' You're not heavy. I can bear your load.

We stop off for a drink at one of the oldest pubs in Cape Town. I feel as if I am inside an old black and white film with the only colors being you and my acorns on the table. I don't want to force conversation; I just want to spend this time accepting each grainy film frame for what it is. We are the only actors in my film as we head back up the steep hill to your house and make love in the late afternoon light. It is strange how easily we can still make love; as if it's the most ordinary thing to do. A fragment of purity despite the dismal state of affairs.

We watch a bizarre art film in bed with wine and cigarettes. When the film ends, I find myself crying uncontrollably. This was not my intention. I was supposed to keep it together; to cheer you up. You visibly withdraw and walk out to sit on the veranda. I know that you are tired of making people miserable so I clumsily try to defend my tears with something from the film. Unable to help myself though, more words spill out. I confess that I'm not coping at home on my own. You lighten up and ask if there is anything you can do to make it better. Just talk. I want to talk. My tears become a means of opportunity to say all the things I may never have another chance to say. I express that I have no regrets about anything that has happened between us and that I consider myself fortunate to have been a part of your life. As dreadful as the last year has been, I thank you for the part you have played in my personal growth. I tell you that I forgive you for everything. I also insist that no matter what happens – my unconditional love for you will never change. It is a relief to say these things. A weight lifts from me and floats out into the sizzling evening air.

In the course of the conversation, I admit that Ruth and I have considered locking you away to be force medicated for your own safety. You have several comments about this. Firstly, you clarify that you would never take medication for any reason. No antiretroviral tablets if you had AIDs, no chemotherapy if you had cancer, and no medication now for depression. Secondly, you confirm that if you were institutionalized, you would kill yourself inside there. When I mention that you might be in a straight jacket, you add, "Well then I'd just bang my head against the wall until I bled to death."

I beg you to reconsider your options. As selfish as it sounds, the girls and I will be left destitute without your income and I don't know how we would survive. I plead with you not to feel as if you have to go through with your threats because you said you would. For once, for god's sake, don't be a man of your word. You state that you are okay and aren't planning anything. I needn't worry as you will continue supporting us. Then we loosen up and make small talk for a while before bed. So far, my suicide watch is going okay. I think.

40

On Monday morning, you go to work and I launch into cleaning the house. You are usually so meticulous and its unkempt state shocks me. The maggots I discover in your tea bag holder make me grimace; a tragic reminder of your decaying condition. After a thorough mop and clean, I walk down to Long Street with a reckless plot to get my first tattoo. My reasoning is that this is something I said I'd never do. It's a part of giving up my relentless responsibility and realizing that I can't always be in control. Worrying about what it will look like in thirty years' time is unimportant. The only thing that is significant is here and now. It's all I have.

My first stop is the Internet cafe for Leila to check messages. I search the Internet for a meaningful symbol for my tattoo. Almost immediately I come across it – the symbol for infinity. A figure 8 with no beginning and no end, a constant cycle; death is merely a transformation of existence. I feel foolish in the tattoo parlor full of brutish men and tattoo connoisseurs. The process is extremely painful, but afterwards, I feel liberated.

I stop in to buy beads and cord to make gifts for the girls on my way to meet Ruth for lunch. We knock back wine in the middle of the day for hours mulling over all our options yet again. We revisit the possibility of involuntary admission to save your life. I share with Ruth what you had to say about that.

You'd kill yourself on the inside. Once again, we are left feeling helpless. Alone.

The sun is setting when I hike back up the steep hill to your house. Pouring another glass of wine, I sit down and start threading beads for the girls while listening to you on the guitar. I think about the appealing notion of moving to a remote part of the world where I can escape to a simple life with no worries. You interrupt my preoccupied thoughts by asking for a piece of cord. Then taking some beads out of your back pack, you thread them and give me a necklace. The beads have different letters on them and the words spell out *T-R-Y H-A-R-D-E-R*. This is puzzling but seeing as you don't explain, I put it into my bag without commenting. After a shower, we investigate my new tattoo and head to watch another film with more wine and cigarettes in bed. This is my last night. We are both aware that we need to transform the grave ambiance. It's an entertaining film and you keep on nudging me and pointing enthusiastically at your favorite parts. I can't bring to mind the last time I saw you laugh like this. For a moment, it is like old times.

After a last cigarette on the veranda, with no moon over the Bo Kaap, we head to bed. Street-lights peek through the tiny gaps in the blinds into the darkness. Just before I drift off, you reach your arm across the bed and clasp my hand. I hold your hand and don't let go. This is how I remember falling asleep. Holding your hand; holding your heart. And hoping that somehow this is the hand I will always hold. I breathe you into my chest. I breathe for you. With you.

The smell of coffee you set next to the bed wakes me. I never heard you get up. Now you are all ready to go to work. I am leaving today; leaving the Bo Kaap, leaving you. I have to go, of course; back to the girls, back to my life. But part of me wants to remain here. Through sleepy eyes, I detect something unusual about your demeanor. Is it the blue-and-white-striped shirt that you are wearing or is it a spark in your transparent blue eyes? You are smiling. I sit up, wanting to delay the moment but you come to kiss me goodbye. I tell you firmly that I'll see you again soon and want to add that I love you, but don't; you know this anyway. Instead, I give you a brave smile. Drinking my coffee alone, I listen to you locking the door and walking down the steps. The gate creaks open and then closed. In my mind, I can see your familiar walk down the hill of the Bo Kaap as you head to work. Feeling a little more optimistic, I dress and pack my bags before going for a last visit to the Internet cafe on Long Street. There is a message from my friend in London telling me that a CD has arrived in the post for Leila.

From: 'Leila Summers'
To: 'Stuart'
Sent: 20 February 2007 10:41 AM

<attached – Ode to a Lemon by Pablo Neruda>

From: 'Stuart'
To: 'Leila Summers'
Sent: 20 February 2007 11:06 AM

Oh, Leila – and I thought I knew all Neruda's poems...

You will know "It happens that I am tired of being a man..." and "Tonight I can write the saddest lines..." and EE Cummings and Anne Sexton and Octavio Paz.

Am reading Annie Proulx's Accordion Crimes and Saul Bellow's More Die of Heartbreak and Martin Amis' Heavy Water (see "Let me Count the Times" and "Denton's Death").

I bite my nails and have had too much coffee this morning and the newsroom is violent today with cussing and unattractive people getting their way.

<attached – poem by E.E. Cummings and Rainer Maria Rilke>

From: 'Leila Summers'
To: 'Stuart'
Sent: 20 February 2007 11:38 PM

Stuart

Your CD arrived today! I think your music is beautiful beyond words. Thank you for sharing it with me. I would like to send you something one day in return, please forward your address.

There is certainly something about Pablo Neruda. I re-read Walking Around and Tonight I Can Write. Apt. As for EE Cummings, I am unconvinced, I might prefer your poetry.

Leila

When Ruth collects me later from your house, she comments on how you unexpectedly arrived at work in a good mood this morning. I joke about the fact that perhaps you are happy that I am leaving. We agree that the other possibility is that things might be looking up. At the airport, I hug her goodbye and wish her luck for her watch.

I can hardly wait to see Jane and Rose again. They don't know I have been in Cape Town. This trip was something I had to do on my own. They could never be expected to understand.

41

From: 'Stuart'
To: 'Robyn'
Sent: 20 February 2007 05:58 PM

Thank you for coming to see me – it is always good to see and talk to you. Love to the girls. x

---

From: 'Robyn'
To: 'Stuart'
Sent: 21 February 2007 09:31 AM

Thank you for talks and tears and touch and cigarettes in bed. I am filled with dread at being home, but managing. The girls will arrive home this morning; I am looking forward to seeing them. I messaged Barry as you suggested saying you were okay. Are you alright?

xx

From: 'Stuart'
To: 'Robyn'
Sent: 21 February 2007 09:55 AM

I'm okay, tired, sleepless. Love the girls. x

For the first two days, I relax a little. It's consoling to have the girls near again. A dear old friend of yours, Mark, is coming to stay with you for a few days. Ruth has updated him and he has offered to take over suicide watch. I am able to make substantial progress with my tax forms. On day three when Mark arrives in Cape Town, Ruth rings to report that you are glum again.

From: 'Stuart'
To: 'Robyn'
Sent: 22 February 2007 11:23 AM

Can you put some money into my account, if any? My pin number, if you ever need it is 4601.

I am not sure about driving to a wedding up country tomorrow. I'll be four hours away from home. That's four hours away from an airport. I argue with myself that my life can't be put on perpetual hold just in case you need me. I must force myself to go to the wedding. Besides, I said I would go. I read your message again. The words 'if you ever need it' jump out at me. I pace back and forth – should I go, shouldn't I go. I suspect that this is a critical time.

A baffling fury emerges within me. Anger I have not identified up to this point. I think I am angry because we are losing you. And there's not a damn thing Ruth or I can do about it. So my anger turns towards the only person you said could save you. Amanda. I am fuming for no other reason than she has not made an effort. While Ruth and I have spent months desperately doing everything in our capability to help you, Amanda who claims to love you, seems to have stepped out of the picture. I certainly can't blame her for the state you have gotten yourself into or how you reacted to the relationship. I am only angry with her for not being honest and for not being there for you. I must do something, but what more can I do? I need to speak to Barry and Amanda.

From: 'Robyn'
To: 'Stuart'
Sent: 22 February 2007 03:11 PM

Hi Stu

I am thinking of calling a meeting with Barry and Amanda. I feel that things have got completely out of control and I think I need to take action. Maybe tonight? I am off to the mountains tomorrow till Tuesday. Chat to you later, probably before you end work. x

---

From: 'Stuart'
To: 'Robyn'
Sent: 22 February 2007 03:14 PM

I suggest just letting Barry and Amanda get on with their lives. Let it go. Love the girls.

From: 'Robyn'
To: 'Stuart'
Sent: 22 February 2007 05:21 PM

I don't know if I should let this go. It's never going to go away. The girls have already lost their dad and we may all lose you now. I have sent Barry a message. If you have any compelling reasons why I shouldn't do this, please… speak…

From: 'Stuart'
To: 'Robyn'
Sent: 22 February 2007 05:25 PM

Do as you please.

From: 'Robyn'
To: 'Stuart'
Sent: 22 February 2007 05:43 PM

I've just put money into your account. Hope your weekend is okay. Phone me on my cell phone if you need anything. I'm sorry I'm angry, but I'm actually fed up now. Things are poked and I feel that Amanda needs to start acting with some integrity. I don't know what I have been thinking being so nice. x

---

From: 'Stuart'
To: 'Robyn'
Sent: 22 February 2007 05:46 PM

She is, believe it or not, my friend.

From: 'Robyn'
To: 'Stuart'
Sent: 22 February 2007 05:52 PM

That's what I've always tried to believe, but some friend. Nice friend to come rushing down to see you when you nearly died. Nice friend to keep contact with you when you lost your entire life for her. Nice friend to NOT consider coming to the mountains when you needed her without me asking her to go, should I go on?

Maybe I will, nice friend to make a million dreamy promises about building a life with you and never for a minute actually mean to go through with any of them. Nice friend to lie about all of it to Barry making you look like the rogue. Nice friend to NOT give a shit!

I am, believe it or not, your friend!

From: 'Stuart'
To: 'Robyn'
Sent: 22 February 2007 05:56 PM

Yes, you are my friend. And I am grateful. She never intended to 'build a life with me.' That's just another of my million unrelated delusions.

From: 'Robyn'
To: 'Stuart'
Sent: 22 February 2007 06:00 PM

I'm sorry for everything, my darling Stuart.

I send you love and good thoughts. x

Barry agrees to meet with me alone at a bar. We drink red wine while discussing everything that has happened. He assures me that I needn't be concerned. He is working on his marriage. He also suspects that you will never end your life. It is frustrating to have him underplay the obvious drama that I am experiencing.

I insist that Amanda needs to spell it out to you that she is not coming. She should then cut contact and let you get on with your life. We talk about Amanda's childhood. When she was a young girl, her teenage brother killed himself. She has never recovered. I suspect that she has spent years trying to fill the gap with other men. I sigh as I begin to comprehend her rock and her hard place. If she did tell you that it was over, she was probably terrified that you would end your life. Either way, she couldn't face feeling responsible for another man's death. From this place, her noncommittal approach makes some sense.

I come home late and drunk and with no resolve. If I can't keep you here for a while longer, maybe Leila can. She is our only hope now.

From: 'Leila Summers'
To: 'Stuart'
Sent: 21 February 2007 03:47 PM

Hi Stuart

I feel a little rude. I want to know all about you and ask you so many tiresome questions but have made little effort to reveal anything about myself.

I live alone apart from my dear cat, Francis, who is the unwilling recipient of all my thoughts. I don't go out much. The world is too big. Apart from that, I read a lot yet still have too many unanswered questions. I have what some call a "fuck buddy" who visits from time to time. I fall in love every day, but with no one in particular. I like being alone, I think.

I am busy reading a book called Memories of My Melancholy Whores by Marquez.

I appreciate your words.

Leila

From: 'Stuart'
To: 'Leila Summers'
Sent: 21 February 2007 04:48 PM

Blessed be Francis. I am writing a short story called "The Entitlement Class", where the unfortunate hero is forced by his longsuffering friends to seek "professional help" and signs up for an "entitlement class". He is paired off with an equally unattractive person (aren't disentitlement and beauty such comfy bedfellows?). It will end badly and I look forward to getting to that part.

"Melancholy whores"– his last book. I felt it showed his age – not by his association with an underage hooker, but just in the writing. He is the bomb and I take much comfort rereading his books. (The construction worker who was so in love, a cloud of yellow butterflies followed wherever he went.) Attached are some photos of a popular big-band I wrote all the music for and awkwardly fronted and Amanda, the woman I will die for. I am lonely.

From: 'Leila Summers'
To: 'Stuart'
Sent: 21 February 2007 08:30 PM

Stuart

I have had too much whiskey and now I talk too much. Sad people are boring, so I prefer to be a recluse. Will you really die for your love when you have her love in return? She is beautiful. Convince me why that would be an option.

White horses.

From: 'Stuart'
To: 'Leila Summers'
Sent: 22 February 2007 09:02 AM

Hello whisky-you.

No, I will not convince you of anything; I am tired of talking and confusing, upsetting people. However, if, for some reason, you find there are no replies to your mail, then it is done. Can we not discuss this any longer?

I am tired; I have an old friend staying with me – another "look after Stuart" plan that my family are secretly putting in place around me. (It surfaced that there was a ball hair's breadth of having me "put away." I think that it was just my past sentiment that I will forever hate anyone that endorses this that stopped that, and now I have a string of do-gooders living on my veranda.) He's sweet, a caustic and fragile sociologist professor who drinks too much, talks too much and is, no doubt, still asleep on my spare bed at home. I got very still last night listening to Jacques Brel sing his *Ne Me Quitte Pas*; it is so beautiful, I wish I didn't have to read a translation to understand it. I haven't brought any lunch to work today and will eat cigarettes instead. I love cigarettes; there is a tobacconist off the market square here that smells like the scalp of someone who has been sleeping for years in clean hay next to his boots. Sometimes I get irritated to have to go to sleep because then it means I can't smoke for a while.

Attached is an article I wrote that you may find some familiarity in...

Stuart

From: 'Leila Summers'
To: 'Stuart'
Sent: 23 February 2007 09:32 AM

Hello Stuart

Okay, Mum's the Word! A sleep tossed night has left me exhausted.

Leila

42

The wedding is a four-hour drive north of Durban. Annie, my old friend who now lives in New Zealand, is finally getting married to her first love. On the way, I deliver the girls to your parents who will be taking them to stay at a hotel in the mountains for five days. After the wedding, I have arranged to join them there.

On my own at last, I drive in silence. The week has been tough, keeping up a face of normality for the girls. Never-ending sparse scenery moves past me. The road seems endless. The further I go, the more I wonder what on earth I am doing. It's too far away from you. I try to calm myself with the fact that today and tomorrow you will be at work with Ruth. Mark is staying at your house and will be there on Sunday, your day off. But today is Friday. I try to cheer up; tonight I can drink and dance.

Eventually I arrive at the hotel and freshen up in my room. Once the church thing is over, I am thankful for a glass of champagne. Sitting outside and smoking cigarettes, I keep my bag close to me. My cell phone is switched to vibrate. Even though you never phone, I expect a call. I know something isn't right. It's just a feeling I have. After a few more glasses of champagne, I settle down a little and do my best to act normal and appear as if I am having fun. I don't want to ruin my friend's wedding.

The dinner tables are sprinkled with green iridescent Paua sea shells. Someone explains to me that the Maori tribes believe they have the power to ward off misfortune. I collect a handful and put them into my handbag.

My crazy friend Lisa is the only person I know at the wedding besides the bride. Once the music starts, I take off my shoes and begin to dance with her. I dance and check my phone. I smoke and check my phone. I would like to ring Ruth but don't want to upset her. Instead, I go to the bathroom and dial your home number. It is nine-thirty p.m. There is no answer. You never answer your home phone; using it only for messages. I leave one saying, "Hello my darling, I am at the wedding in Newcastle. I am drinking champagne – *giggle* – and dancing and all I can think about is you. I should be having fun, but I am worried about you tonight. So for some reason, I wanted to phone and tell you that I send you lots and lots of love and light and I'm thinking about you. I love you Stuart. Always know that."

I hang up and go outside for another smoke. I know you won't call me back but still I check constantly. No one calls. I dance all night. My body doesn't want to, but I force it to move to the music.

Far away in Cape Town, Ruth is also at a party. She is just as worried. She is also dancing. She leaves you a message on your phone around the same time I do.

At three a.m. I am the last one to leave the party. Back in my strange musty hotel room, I collapse in my clothes on top of the bed. All I think about is finding an Internet cafe first thing in the morning. Leila needs to check her mail.

On my way to meet the bride and some of the others for breakfast, I drive through the small town in search of an Internet cafe. As it turns out, I find one and it is open all day. Leila checks her messages to find a brief one you sent yesterday morning. Still, I am relieved to see it. Any words let me know that you are still around. I compose a reply from Leila and then head off to breakfast planning to return afterwards to read your response.

From: 'Stuart'
To: 'Leila Summers'
Sent: 23 February 2007 09:34 AM

Hello.

I posted off a compilation of other songs of mine to you this morning – surface mail; will be with you in 2010...

Be rested, my friend.

From: 'Leila Summers'
To: 'Stuart'
Sent: 24 February 2007 10:35 AM

Hi Stuart

Another CD, thank you, I look forward to this. I ask again for your address. I have something silly and small to send you.

Last night I attended a large dinner party and fell in love with a quiet shy man across the other side of the room. We eyed each other out all evening (or was that my imagination?). Strange thing is, I never wanted to speak to him, I never dreamed of having sex with him. I just wanted to look at him across the room and imagine that he was who I thought he could be. There was a rather annoying foreigner who insisted on following me around all night and prying into my life. He was sweet enough, and I could have taken him home like a lost puppy dog, but that would have just been sex.

Aren't we strange creatures? I was happy with the 'love' without one word rather than contemplating the sex without any 'love.' I don't understand these things at all. But I had a pleasant evening with far too much alcohol. Maybe that's it.

Leila

Breakfast is bland and I am aware of the slow passing of time. One o'clock seems too far away; the time you are expected to start work. You will probably arrive hung over and tired to sit down next to Ruth who will hand you a packed lunch. I know the first thing you will do is check your messages. Then you will respond to Leila.

I arrive back at the Internet café at ten to one. All the computers are taken. I don't mind waiting. I get out my cell phone and ring your father to make plans for meeting up with them this afternoon at their hotel in the mountains. He answers. I start to give details of when I will arrive. He interrupts me. He repeats my name three times before I stop talking mid-sentence. There is urgency in his voice. In the tiny pause of his breath, I know. I know what he is about to tell me. He says it anyway.

"It's over, Robyn. Stuart is dead."

I stop moving. Everything stands still. I am alone in a tiny run-down Internet cafe in the middle of a strange town. Leila is about to send you a message. You can't be dead. Your father is still speaking. He explains that a hospital in Cape Town had phoned him. The doctors tried everything, but it was too late; you didn't make it. You drowned. That's all he knows. He had phoned Ruth and was about to ring me when I called. I listen. He lets me know that they are packing and leaving the mountains right away to go home. He had to tell the girls because they needed to understand the sudden change of plans. He says they seem fine. All I can manage to say is that I am so sorry. I will meet them at their home; I can be there in three hours. I swallow, put down the phone, and turn to the man standing behind the desk.

"Thank you, I no longer need to use the computer."

PART V

43

On the dusty street outside the Internet cafe, I open the door of my car and fall inside. My body is trembling feverishly. At a loss about what to do next, I just wait for a while in total shock. Although the eventuality of this moment has gone around in my mind many times before, I am not ready. My vision blurs and I struggle for breath. There is no air in the car. For a giddy second, the idea that I might still be asleep in the hotel room seizes me. But this vanishes in an instant as the busy street racket draws me back to reality along with the echoing words – It's over, Robyn.

Fortunately, I remember that Lisa could still be in town. My unsteady fingers dial her phone number. As I arrive at her hotel, she is waiting outside and begins running towards me. Climbing numbly out of the car, I collapse gratefully into her open arms. She holds me up as my body shudders with sobs. For the second time, Lisa is at my side at a time of calamity. I crash down on the grass and welcome the strong cup of coffee and sugar water she hands me. The air is warm and motionless. A yellow butterfly on a nearby shrub waves its wings gently at me. I gaze at it until it flutters out of view and remember reading that some butterflies live for only five days. Such a short time for such intoxicating beauty. It was five days ago that I left you; smiling.

I take another sip of bitter coffee before ringing Ruth. As she answers, we both begin to cry. Ruth was driving to work with a neatly packed lunch for you when she got the call from your father. She pulled over and parked on the side of a road she doesn't recognize. We attempt to console each other with the fact that you are at peace now. There are no details yet, only that you are gone. Ruth is appreciative when I volunteer to be the one to let Amanda know.

Just before I leave on my long drive, Lisa hands me a pack of cigarettes and some money. She folds her arms around me, as I make my last phone call. Amanda answers and immediately asks if everything is okay.

"No. Nothing is okay," I announce sadly. "Stuart drowned this morning, Amanda." She gasps sharply as I continue, "We don't know any details yet. I just want you to know that this is no one's fault." She is wheezing so heavily that she only manages a mumbled apology before hanging up.

The highway is not far off. Once I'm in the car, I send a brief text message to my family and friends to let them all know. Susie calls right away to offer condolences, adding; "Now you can begin to work on yourself." I think this is a truly bizarre thing to say to someone who has just lost their husband, but I choose to ignore it. When I try to answer the next call, all I get is a long beep; like a medical flat line. My phone dies, leaving me without any contact to the outside world. It's probably best; I need some time alone. The phone never works again.

Turning up the radio, I drive the monotonous road and as the landscape passes me by, so does my life; my time with you. The melodic lyrics of a song *How to Save a Life* by The Fray capture my attention – 'Where did I go wrong, I lost a friend, somewhere along in the bitterness and I would have stayed up with you all night, had I known how to save a life…'

Suddenly I get goose bumps as I clearly experience your presence in the car. I glance into the rearview mirror and then slowly turn around, expecting to see a ghost. But I can't see you. A glorious golden light peeks out from behind the clouds and an incredible sense of calm wraps around me. I manage a smile as I say out loud, "You made it, Stu." I get the strong feeling that you are somehow impressing on me that you are at peace now.

I think about how I drove this same road yesterday in the opposite direction. Last night while Ruth and I danced and drank, I imagine you were packing up your house methodically. Two messages would have been flashing on your answering machine as you deleted everything off your computer, threw your secrets away and polished your shoes. Messages from two different women connected by a similar panic and united by a love for you. I wonder if you listened to the messages. You would not have been able to talk to anyone. There would have been nothing left to say. Your mind was made up.

Three hours later I arrive at your parent's house. Turning off the ignition, I hesitate to collect myself before going inside. My girls! What will I say to my darling girls? How can they be expected to understand? I can't yet comprehend that you are gone.

Your whole family is inside: your parents, your older brother and his wife and your youngest sister Rachel. Everyone is here except for Ruth. Jane and Rose are playing outside. "Hello Mommy," they announce rather cheerfully. I offer a weak smile and hug them without saying anything.

After hugging everyone, I excuse myself to book air tickets to Cape Town for the morning. Afterwards, I join the adults on the veranda and we begin the practical business of discussing funeral arrangements. When I mention that I have already contacted a funeral parlor in Cape Town, your father stares at me in astonishment. I had to be organized. I knew. I am calm. Someone hands me a glass of wine. I drink it. Jane runs over and says, "Mommy why is Granny crying, when Dad is so happy in heaven?"

I gently explain that it's because it is still very sad for those of us left here on earth. Your sister Rachel is angry. She is angry at God. Gulping my wine I remind her that we all have a free will. You chose the only option you felt you had under the circumstances.

After another hour-long drive home, I wearily carry the suitcases inside and repack them for a fourth trip to Cape Town in two months. Only this time, you won't be there; just a lifeless body. I feed the animals and then climb into bed with a little girl on each side. We talk about heaven and how wonderful it must be. They ask me to read a section from my Sylvia Browne book on 'the other side.' I've read it to them before, but I read it again and sing them the lullaby.

Once they are asleep, I attempt to get up and find that the air feels solid. It's an effort to move. I start shaking again and my skin is burning. I wonder where your body is. What it looks like. How cold it is. I light a cigarette on the veranda and the tears come. So much water. You will not cry again. I will. I believe I will never stop. Carrying my bones to bed, I huddle in between the girls in my clothes. I have a plane to catch in the morning. I lie frozen until sleep finds me.

44

On Sunday night, Ruth and I sit under the trees with a bottle of red wine and attempt to swallow the fact that you are gone. The girls are watching a movie in the house with Bradley. Earlier today I called the state hospital where you were proclaimed dead. All they could tell me was that you arrived by ambulance in a state of profound hypothermia and after failed attempts at resuscitation, you were declared deceased. They gave me the name and phone number of the paramedic who was on duty at the time. I haven't called him yet. Your body lies in the Salt River state morgue and we will have to go there tomorrow to find out what we need to do.

A warm breeze rustles the leaves. There are still a few hours before the summer sun sets at nine o'clock in Cape Town. The piercing ring of the doorbell makes Ruth and I cringe. We don't want to see anyone yet; to have to try and explain is unthinkable. We ignore it in the hope that whoever it is will go away. But the bell rings persistently. Irritated, Bradley answers the door. Michelle barges her way past him and heads straight for us. Michelle is the wife of one of your oldest friends. She is fragile and has spent the last few years in and out of psychiatric hospitals. As long as she takes her medication and stays off the booze, she manages. She hands me a package and sits down, uninvited. Her scraggly blond hair clings to her face and mascara bleeds down from her red, bulging eyes. She reaches across and helps herself to my glass of wine. Gulping it down, she glares at Ruth and me, demanding to know why we look so calm. When she has polished off my wine, she moves onto Ruth's.

Michelle rants about how she cannot believe you are dead. She maintains that we couldn't possibly be sure that it is you if we haven't been to see the body. She requests to come along to the morgue with us in the morning. As gently as we can, Ruth and I respond that this is something we prefer to do alone. Her presence and comments are inherently offensive and Ruth finally gets pissed off. She hisses at Michelle that her fucking brother has just died before storming off to submerge herself in the bath. I'm left sitting with Michelle and no more wine. She leans in towards me, and gripping my arm, whines that I don't know how much she loved you.

Actually, I do know. You told me that you had seen her a few times recently, drunk and out of control. During one of these episodes she admitted, in front of her husband, that she had always harbored feelings for you. I sigh and say that I'm sure you adored her too. Finally she screeches off in her car after insisting that the wrapped package she brought be cremated with your body. Ruth and I later open the package to find it contains a pair of red high-heeled shoes along with some poems and photographs.

That night I have a vivid dream. I dream that you are sitting in an armchair across from me in an empty room. You seem peaceful and it feels as though we communicate for hours. I'm not sure of all that is said between us, only that you impress on me that everything is okay now.

Michelle's husband rings me early the next morning to inform us that we no longer need to go and identify your body. He explains that he and Michelle had gone to the morgue late last night. What?! I specifically informed her that this was something that Ruth and I needed to do. He apologizes and groans that he couldn't stop her and so he felt it was better to accompany her under the circumstances. Questions race through my mind. Why did the morgue let them in on a Sunday night? Why would they let a non-family member identify a body? He remarks that you don't look too good, and in a way maybe it is better that we don't see you. I am speechless. I feel so invaded. Ruth is fuming too. I immediately call the morgue. The attendant on duty knows nothing about it. He maintains that no paperwork has been done and that the body is, as yet, unidentified. He concludes that we still need to take care of it. After breakfast, Ruth and I leave the girls at a child care recreation center and follow the directions to the Salt River state morgue.

In the waiting room, the stench of decay is strong under the air conditioners. We move to the other side of the room where it is only marginally better. Around us, scattered family members are crying. Ruth and I are wobbly, preparing ourselves for what is ahead. At long last our number is called. We follow a man in a white coat down a poorly lit passage to a small room where he leaves us alone. In front of us is a thick glass window and we watch as the curtain on the other side is drawn open. Your body is covered with a white sheet and lies on a metal table. I inhale and hold in the air as the sheet is pulled back to reveal your head. Your face is a little contorted and your eyes are squeezed tightly shut. There are several tubes jammed inside your mouth. I grip Ruth's arm and escort her out of the room. I've seen all I need to see. It is undeniably you.

We are led to an office where I have to fill in some forms and provide a thumbprint. The fingerprinting device is not working, and the novice clerk is getting frustrated. Ruth and I giggle nervously. The clerk gives us a strange look, no doubt because he is used to family members crying rather than smiling. When the clerk leaves the room to find a working device, Ruth and I sneak a peek at the open file on the desk. There is nothing telling on the police report. It takes about twenty minutes to obtain a thumbprint they can use. Afterwards, we race out of there, wanting to go as far away as possible from the horrifying place.

That afternoon, I telephone the paramedic who was on ambulance duty at the time of your drowning. He is kind and offers his sincere condolences. He informs me that some time after eleven in the morning, two deep sea divers found your body floating in the sea. They pulled you onto the shore and provided mouth to mouth resuscitation for about half an hour before he arrived in the ambulance. You were then rushed to the state hospital. The reason you were not yet pronounced dead was due to your extremely low body temperature. He explains that, in a state of profound hypothermia, a person's heart rate may become so slow that a pulse cannot be detected. A person can therefore not be declared dead until their body is warmed. He left you at the hospital where I have already found out that, after various attempts to warm and revive you failed, the doctor on duty proclaimed you deceased around twelve thirty. When I ask the paramedic if he believes you died out in the sea he speculates that is most likely what happened. I feel somewhat better. You wanted to die at sea, not in a hospital.

45

I unlock the front door to your house with the spare keys I kept from my last visit with you. I left them with Ruth in case we needed them. Yesterday, after your mom arrived, we all came here together. Jane and Rose ran around the house exploring and choosing items they wanted to keep. Jane chose your dictaphone and Rose claimed your alarm clock. Your mom lay on your bed smelling your pillow and crying while Ruth and I searched for any clues. We found nothing; no letters of love or pain.

Today, I need to be in your house on my own for a while before we start packing up. I want to feel, look, think. I wander around slowly. You never felt this was home, but it still feels like you. Everything is neat and tidy. The dishes are washed; your shoes are neatly lined up. Not a trace of the turmoil. Your bed is roughly made and one used tea cup sits on the kitchen counter next to a book of hand-written poetry. Neatly tucked under the book was a fifty Rand note; money you owed to Ruth. I try to imagine what you did, how you felt. Did it matter to you that this was the last cup of tea you would ever drink? I walk over to the accordion box and open it again. Maybe we missed something yesterday. But everything is the same. In my mind, I hear your music.

You were alive. Your body walked to the beach that day or maybe you hitched. You left your blue motorbike sinking into the hot melting tar outside your house. You were alive. You loved to ride your motorbike, but that day you walked. Did you leave your motorbike here for me to find it? What were you thinking about as your feet loped in large uneven strides or was it dragging soles or hesitant steps? Were you determined as you walked with intent or did you falter? Did you walk slowly, wanting to think for the last time; to take in the world that you were leaving? Did you smile and nod to a beggar as you usually did, shouting 'ello' as you waved? By that time, you wouldn't have been able to bear thinking about the girls. They were the one thing that could hold you back from where you were determined to go. But I suspect they would have been on your mind nonetheless. That would have been the hardest part for you. When you reached your destination, you would have walked along the sand and sat on the rocks smoking cigarettes. You were alive. You walked, you thought, you sat, you smoked. I wonder, did you cry? Was it, like the last time, the most peaceful day of your life? I suspect you swallowed at least a hundred sleeping pills again before swimming out into the clear ocean. How far did you swim? You were alive. You had a heart with such capacity for love, yet also for pain. You had a brain that I have, on occasion, questioned whether it had a chemical imbalance. Was that true? Or was it only the angst of your mind and emotions that caused your intense suffering? I will never know.

Once I've been in your house for long enough, I come outside onto the veranda where I sit down in my gray chair. The same place I sat just over a week back with you. I roll a cigarette with the tobacco that was left in your bag. The bag was handed over to me at the morgue after being found abandoned on the rocks. Ruth and I had taken it back to her house where we sat down and lit a cigarette before opening it. Slowly we peered inside as if it were a crucial piece of evidence. It looked as it always did, except that it mistakenly contained someone else's underpants and socks. Ruth and I, disgusted, quickly put them in the outside bin. Some other poor grieving family will be missing them. We looked through everything in your bag as if it were sacred but found nothing remarkable. The only thing that was different was your key ring, which you had changed since I last visited. It now contained one of the girls' toys, a ladybug.

Your tobacco, your house, your poems… everything is here except for you, although it still feels as if you could be. It is unfathomable. You should be here, smoking your tobacco with me on your veranda. When I can no longer stand it, I go back to Ruth's house, back to our girls.

46

From the top of Table Mountain in Cape Town, I can make out the beach where you drowned. The girls have gone for a walk with your mom and I sit alone under the shade of a rock, smoking a cigarette. In the distance the vast emerald ocean looks alive with lashing foam sprays near the shoreline. I can't quite make out any details from so high up, but I believe that I see the straight silhouette of the wings of an albatross soaring above the sea. You are flying free.

Amanda is in Cape Town. You had always hoped she would

come. You waited for her. I remember you said that you saw her in every girl. When someone looked particularly similar to her, you'd fall in love with them immediately and that would make you cry. You kept imagining that Amanda would come around the corner in her sunglasses as you sat and drank a cappuccino; that she'd come because she, too, knew she couldn't live without you. She is here now. But it's too late.

Your body is laid out neatly in the funeral parlor. It has been moved here from the morgue after your post-mortem. Ruth and I aren't sure we will view it, but your mom wants this. She hasn't seen you in over a year.

A few days ago Barry called me to say that Amanda wanted to come to Cape Town. She wants to see your body. This has been difficult to arrange without letting your mom know. I have explained to the compassionate woman at the funeral parlor that once we leave, a close friend of yours will be coming for a second viewing. She is aware that she can't mention this to your mom as it will upset her.

We arrive at the small building in an industrial area across the road from a cemetery. The woman takes your mom into the viewing room while Ruth and I stay in the waiting area. After a time, we both decide that we may as well go inside. Your body lies in a coffin, covered completely except for your face. You look as if you are sleeping peacefully. I see your body but you are not here. Underneath the sheet, I think about how your body is cut to pieces from the post-mortem. I look away. The woman has a soothing look. Your mom is weeping. She touches your face lightly and cries out, "My baby!" A candle burns and the woman utters a prayer as the three of us embrace.

Barry and Amanda have been waiting in their car around the corner. As we leave, I send a text message to let them know that they can go inside. I wonder how Amanda will feel as she stands in that strange room looking at your lifeless face.

The following day you are cremated. I collect your ashes in a modest box. For our last few days in Cape Town, the girls carry the box of ashes around the house, chatting to you and telling you what they are doing.

Ruth travels home with us to Durban for your wake. The following day your family, the girls, and I take your ashes out in a boat and scatter them in the Durban harbor. I always wanted to bring you home, but not in a small plastic bag. Ruth reads a poem. The girls throw crystals into the water. Then we go to your wake, which I have organized at a clubhouse on one of your favorite beaches. A large gathering of family and friends arrive and drink copious amounts of alcohol. The two songs that you requested in your will are played. One of them is Moon River. I remember that was the song that was played on the violin at our wedding. Jane dances to the music. She says we are celebrating your life. Friends cry. Your mom cries. I don't seem to have any tears left.

Jane and Rose dictate their memories of the day to me.

"Dad, I know you died, don't be sad because only your body died. I love you so don't be sad. I remember when we got out of the bath, you dropped us on the bed and I bounced up and then I dropped down. I thought it was fun. I love you Dad. When we went on the boat trip then we throwed Daddy's ashes in. It was very nice. When Daddy came to the beach he drowned. His body died. Now he's inside our hearts. But there's only one thing, only his body died, he's in heaven. He can do whatever he wants; he's having fun in heaven. And then after that we know he's in our hearts and we know he loves us."

Rose, 4 years old – 12 March 2007

"When I was in Cape Town, me and my mom remembered Dad and we drew a heart for him in the sandpit at the park. Last time my Dad took me to the same park and he swung me and I had so much fun. Yesterday we went on a boat trip with our granny. We sprinkled my Dad's ashes into the sea. After that we threw some crystals into the sea for Dad because we love him. We got off the boat and we went to celebrate my Dad and we had lots of fun. On the way home we saw a restaurant that my Dad once took me up. It was very nice."

Jane, six years old – 12 March 2007

One of your close friends later e-mailed me a story he had written about that day which made me weep.

Farewell at Vetch's Pier
(to Stuart 1968 – 2007)
by Kobus Moolman

Dusk. And the tide was coming in. The waves full and brown and loud. A yellow moon, swollen, above the ocean. Lights coming on in all the windows of the tall hotels all along Marine Parade. Yellow and orange and white lights, across the wide rolling water. Rolling in. Up the white beach. In front of the grimy clubhouse. Under a pallid sky.

The tide was full. And the clubhouse was full. When I arrived. Late, as usual. Dripping with sweat and stinking. Because I had got lost. Because I did not know where I was going. Because I had walked all the way from Addington beach, along the white sand, through the wind that smelled of fish and oil. Slipping and cursing and sweating. Because you were my dear friend. And I did not want to say goodbye. And I could not believe that you were dead.

Dusk. And the tide was full at Vetch's. The beach so beloved by you and that other lover of words both foul and fair, Douglas Livingstone. The tide was brown and loud and full at Captain Vetch's pier. Where, after almost 150 years of wind and sun and spray, the pier might be no more. And the beach too, with its rusted effluent pipe. Its sagging wire fence and scrappy grass and builders' rubble. Just a fancy new marina in their place. With a gondola even. Sailing in a fancy artificial waterway, with a bored black gondolier in a white shirt and waistcoat.

And the clubhouse was full. And everyone was there. Painters and guitarists and violinists and photographers and doctors and drunkards (professional and non) and your wife and your sister and your mother and your father, and everyone was sad and everyone was angry and they were stunned and they were shocked and they kept saying, "I don't believe it. I don't believe it. I don't believe it." Over and over. To themselves. To each other. To you.

And the bare room was full. The bare room with the long bar counter was full and hot and noisy. And everyone was there. And everyone was so much older. So much grayer. Paler. Harder. More tired. And the air was hot. And the air was full of your voice. Of the voice of your guitar and your accordion. Full of the voice of the sea and the voice of everything that the cold sea could not finally drown out. Ever. The small voice of memory.

And I remembered you. And this city. You as angry and gentle as this city. This city as fierce and lonely and beautiful as you. Beautiful as the black waves under the moon. As a woman on the edge of the water with her skirts hitched up high, wading in far, far into the black waves. Lonely as a cargo freighter, heavy and huge, sliding silently up the narrow channel into the harbor. As the thin Indian fisherman and his son who throw hopeful lines into the oily water of the harbor. As the light that flashes red and green and red and green all night on the end of the pier.

And I remembered you and knew that I would never forget. Never ever. For as long as I live. Cross my heart and hope to die, stick my finger in my eye. You. And every mad, bad, beautiful thing we did in this city. When I was younger. When I had hair. Not so long ago. When nothing mattered. Not getting drunk or getting stoned or fighting or dreaming or having money or having none. Not as long as we were alive.

Not dead. Not dead-alive like so many pushing their long years up the long roads that wound through the factories and the warehouses, the shunting yards and the workshops of Montclair and Wentworth, the darkened roads that wound through the darkened Point (then) leading nowhere, the dirt roads of Cato Manor and Kwadebeka and Lamontville with their pools of muddy water (still) standing and their rubbish.

I would never forget the lush green oasis of your corrugated iron house on the Berea, just around the corner from the hospital, in that street I could never find first off. I would never forget the loeries that sang in your garden. That sounded like water rolling between the rocks, underneath and around and between the large-leaved delicious monsters in your garden. I would never forget the moon that sang in your garden between the arms of the pear tree.

But mostly I would never forget, even though I now want to

forget, that time I slept in my car parked at the top of your driveway at five o' clock on a winter morning. Because a violent concoction the long sweet night before of doe-eyed fate and obsession and plain straight-forward betrayal had driven me to a precipice whose open mouth I could not resist. And you had laughed uproariously and made a raucous song out of my guilt and my obsession. But when your turn came . . . There was no laughter. And only heart-rending songs.

And I would never forget and I would always remember. Always. How we fought on the sand in the middle of the night, just outside here. Here. Yes, it must have been. How could I have forgotten? Because we had been drinking. Because we had been arguing. Because it did not matter. Because I had never fought anyone before. Because I, who had always prided myself on the strength of my arms, wanted to prove to myself, to you, how strong I was. And so we wrestled. In the sand. And we rolled and we swore and we laughed. In the sand. Until we were covered in sand. Like children, I suppose, now that I think about it. But it didn't matter. Sand in our eyes, in our ears, in our mouths. Until you pinned me down. In the sand. And I couldn't move. Because you had swimmer's arms and you were heavier. But it didn't matter. Losing or winning, really. Until we got to my car. That little white Jetta, remember? And I didn't have the key. Because the key was buried somewhere in the sand. Somewhere deep in the sand where we had been wrestling. Never to be found again.

But I have never forgotten and I will always remember. Always. What happened after. Because those were the days when I didn't believe in anything. Not God. Not myself. Not the void. Not love. Which was failing, in an empty house in another city eighty miles away, fast. Not my strong arms, which had failed. And I said a silent prayer. And not long after an angel arrived. Dressed in a fisherman's smelly overalls. And he had a metal detector. And he was combing the beach for all the shiny things that people lose or want to leave behind or just plain forget.

But there is so much I have forgotten. And am trying so hard to remember. To write down, somewhere. So that you are not forgotten. So that not one footprint of yours across the sand at Vetch's pier, up and down the fetid alleyways all along the Point, through all the bars and the strip-joints and the late-night crowded nightclubs across this sweltering throbbing city, so that not one footprint of yours or tyre-print of your big old blue BMW motorbike or paw-print of your three-legged dog, Mr. Spooks ("always the first to arrive and the last to leave"), so that not one mark left of your holy and unholy life across this unholy and holy city will ever be forgotten.

But it is dusk now. And the tide is coming in. The tide is full and brown and the air is loud with seagulls and children, and somewhere I hear a woman weeping. The light is fading and the dark water stretches far, far away from your group of ageing friends on the wet sand; so much older than I could have imagined us ever to be. And tired. So very tired of pushing our long years up the long roads . . .

But the lights are coming on in all the windows of the tall hotels all along Marine Parade now. And the shadows have gone from this doomed beach. And I think, earlier, stumbling through a car park and out onto a stinking dune overlooking the clubhouse, I heard your voice. I turned. A gray heron took off from a faded bush.

47

I feel sad to the bone. It is three weeks since you left this world. Up until now, I have managed by keeping busy with organizing all that needed to be done. After the two weeks in Cape Town, Ruth spent a week with us in Durban. She left this morning. The house feels lonely and deserted.

I have the feeling that my life has been good up until now and that I don't need to be here anymore; that it's over. I may as well curl up and disappear with my memories. That would be enough. I could just vanish in a puff. I suppose that's one part of how you felt; only you had the nerve to make yourself vanish.

Taking another sip of coffee, I watch the girls doing woodwork in the garden. The sunlight reflects in their golden curls. It's still warm and humid in Durban, even though autumn has supposedly arrived. With some old planks, some nails, and a hammer, they are building a fairy castle. In their playtime, they appear happy. It's mainly at night that they are thrown into that lonely place without you. I put up a photo of you next to your empty side of the bed. Rose looks at it before she goes to sleep. She misses you terribly. They both do. I know that you are alive in spirit, but I wish you were still here in body. I wish the girls could have had more time with you. Do you know all this? I will talk to you anyway. I will still tell you everything. How I am. How am I?

I don't know how to do this, how to be okay, how to get through. I walk around aimlessly, barely managing to eat or do much else. Friends have been kind and helpful but all the help in the world is never going to make this any better. The days are long and hard. The nights are longer. The girls are the only reason I am here.

The house is full of you. Memories and piles of things are scattered everywhere – your books, your music, your pictures, your CDs. Your newspaper cuttings are in scrapbooks and drawers. The color you painted on the walls, the light fixtures you put up. Outside is your empty rocking chair and next to it the old whiskey barrel you once stole, as well as the plants you planted in the garden and loved to water every night. In the lounge lies an unpacked box of your belongings from Cape Town with the two items of your clothing I chose to keep. The blue-and- white-striped shirt you were wearing on the day I last saw you breathing. And your favorite brown woolen pullover that reminds me of your bear hugs. There are still some things in a box outside that I was getting ready to bring to you in Cape Town, stuff for your new home. You kept warning me to stop bringing your belongings; saying you didn't need them. I knew what you were implying but I wanted to prove you wrong. So I brought as much as I could carry on every visit. I thought that somehow by bringing your possessions I was not going along with your plans not to need them.

I think about the old house next door. If we had bought that property, if you had moved in there instead of moving to Cape Town, would you still be around? I slump down among the boxes and piles of spring cleaning and drop my head between my knees and begin to sob. I can't do this anymore. I can't do any of it.

48

For a whole week before seeing Susie, I spend my time engrossed in making photo albums. I devote hours every night to scanning and printing pictures, determined that the girls need to have a visual history of you; physical memories to prove that we were a family. You never liked having your photograph taken, so it requires some effort to place your presence systematically throughout the girls' years. I buy albums, search through back-up discs for digital photos and dig yellowed envelopes out of drawers. Night by night I re-create our lives together.

Some of the photos I come across are from a time before I met you. I stare at the clear blue eyes of an innocent adolescent dressed in an army uniform. You look so young. I recall stories you told me of how much you hated your time in the army as a medic. You and your fellow medics got up to much mischief – stealing ambulances to go out drinking; taking as many drugs as you had time for, even injecting yourselves with experimental concoctions. At times you would give the sergeants laxatives instead of the medication they came in for. I wonder now why I didn't ask you more about the long scars on your arms. What happened in the army that made you suicidal? I suppose I considered that was in the past; a time when you were young and foolish. I realize now that there were many facts I didn't know or didn't choose to see.

I take the albums I've created to my session with Susie. After explaining to her that this is how I've managed to get through the first few weeks at home, she looks at me and sighs. "So it's still all about Stuart?" she says. "When is it going to start being about you?"

I don't say anything, but inside, I disagree. I've created a legacy for my children, a physical reminder of their dad, and I've managed to keep somewhat sane. This is about me. It's always been about me. This is me. This is my life.

It's chilly and rainy and it seems that autumn might have arrived after all. I've started methodically rewriting my scribbled journal from the past year. It looks as though it could turn into a book. There's so much to tell. I need to write it all down for the girls so that one day, maybe they will understand.

I think of you every minute of every day. I come across haunting reminders everywhere. I cleaned out an old handbag from the last trip to Cape Town and found your set of keys for our house. It hit me once again that you are actually gone. Small things make me want to cry. Yesterday it was the recipe books, which reminded me of all the recipes I had marked out to try but never got a chance to prepare for you. Today I came across a stack of x-rays under a chair. Looking at your chest bones from the time you had the motorbike accident was a chilling reminder that you used to be physically present. I used to be able to put my arms around that chest.

Some days, I don't feel as if my life is real at all. Once I was a seven-year-old girl playing in the endless afternoons. I would dream of life as a real person with a home and herb garden and the smell of sweet jasmine. Then, in what seems like the next instant, I am here. Thirty-seven years old. Old. I look at Jane who is six and Rose who is now five. I wonder who they belong to. I don't feel old enough to have children. Sometimes, they look like strangers and it all seems utterly alien. It is almost as if I am in someone else's house and I've taken over their life for a while. Soon I'll be whisked back in time to when I am seven and still playing happily in the garden waiting to be called in for some pancakes. How on earth did I get from seven to thirty-seven and barely notice it? I am all grown up. I have two children. I have my dream house with herbs and jasmine that has died but will be replanted in the spring in the attempt to live my childhood dreams. I live alone. There is no husband. That was not in my dreams. I am a widow; such a foreign word on my tongue. The concept is too difficult to contemplate. Stuart, sometimes, I just don't believe you did it. I don't believe you are dead.

49

I smell bacon before I open my eyes. It must be coming from next door. I remember waking up late on Sunday mornings to the smell of frying bacon and fresh coffee and the sound of the girls giggling. You would already be home from the beach with the girls and the dogs. One morning you let Jane help you decide which food coloring to add to the scrambled eggs. I was served blue eggs for breakfast. They didn't look particularly appetizing. But we all ate them.

Jane stirs next to me and murmurs, "I miss Dad." Then she smiles sleepily as she describes her dream to me. She dreamt that you came to fetch her on the back of a flying unicorn. She jumped up behind you and you flew around all night showing her a magical world. She exclaims how real it was. I haven't seen a smile so wide on her face for some time now.

For the past two months, I have sensed your presence frequently. The other night I dreamt about you too. I was lying in bed cuddled against you. You were reading. As I nuzzled closer, I looked up and saw your face smiling down at me. That was all there was to the dream, but it was warm and comforting.

The time I felt your presence most vividly was one night when I had the overwhelming sense that you were in the bathroom with me. I turned around slowly, apprehensive that I would find you standing there. Though I couldn't see you, when I was about to walk out of the bathroom naked, I clearly *heard* you say, "I wouldn't do that if I were you." I turned back and wrapped up in a towel. As I came through the bathroom doorway, I saw my neighbor outside the window and grinned at him before dashing into my room. I certainly thanked you for that!

The girls see you more than I do. A while back, Jane asked me why you run next to our car all the time. Trying not to sound too surprised, I asked her what she meant. She explained that every time we drive in the car, you run next to us. She said you must be running fast although it doesn't look like it. Your legs move normally but are a little above the ground. I nonchalantly let her know that it is probably because you had promised to watch over us. Jane sees you often. She says that at times you are your normal size but other times you are very small. She awoke one night and said she couldn't move because the covers of the bed were pressed down next to her, as if someone was sitting there. Rose had a dream that you were a teddy bear. You could appear and disappear and she was the only one that could see you. Twice she told me that you tickled her on the back. The girls both still visit you in their secret places just as Susie taught them to do.

Ruth seems to be the most intuitive. In her dreams, you are frequently playing your guitar with Mr. Spooks by your side.

All this is encouraging, but it isn't enough. I want you here. But not as you were for your final year. It would be selfish of me to want to have you back in that condition, if it meant you must go on suffering as you did. I keep trying to remind myself of the bigger picture. All my grief and questions won't bring you back. One of the greatest gifts is free will and I have to accept that you had yours and respect your wishes to go in peace. I wanted you to be happy, and you weren't. Now maybe you are.

I somehow felt that our journey together would be cut short; that you would die young. I dared to share this with some close friends soon after we were married. Such intensity occasionally comes in spurts that cannot last forever. Rather than trying to go against the grain as some may have thought, you spent your whole life trying to be as normal in society as you could manage. At times, you handled it, but every so often you had to try harder. You knew you wouldn't survive without this huge effort. It must have been tiring for you. Lately you mentioned that you were just extremely tired. A lifetime spent trying. I was confused when you gave me the necklace with the beaded words TRY HARDER. Ruth later informed me that you had bought them for yourself and had pinned them onto your bag as a reminder. That night when you gave me the beads, you must have known you couldn't do it any longer. I keep the necklace hanging next to my bed to remind me that you tried as hard as you could in this world.

From the veranda, the trees thrust shadowy silhouettes into the sky. The moonlight appears through them in dappled contours. I could sit all night and gaze at them. I could sit here and never move again. Nothing seems without effort these days. Moving is an effort. Every now and then I think I hear you whispering that you have no regrets.

You gave me the impossible task of explaining everything to people after you were gone. It's too difficult. The words don't come out right and then I forget what it is that I thought I understood about all this.

50

It takes me three months to decide I must tell the girls that your death wasn't an accident. The question of whether I should reveal the complicated truth has been a constant source of angst and deliberation for me all this time. Susie and others have strongly advised against it, but my heart has continued to pull me in the opposite direction. Not knowing which route to trust, the decision has felt too enormous to make on my own.

But my mind has recently been made up after hearing Jane express regret that a boat didn't sail by to throw you a life saver when you swam out too far in the sea. I don't want them to live with the idea that you could have been saved; that it was all a terrible accident. Nor do I feel comfortable keeping the truth from them. I know that at some point in their lives, they will find out what really happened. Putting myself in their shoes, I can imagine the tremendous shock and hurt they could feel over having been deceived by me, the one person they most needed to be able to trust at this time. I'm not willing to compound their loss in that way. I love them too much to run that risk.

Just before bedtime, I let Jane and Rose know that I have something important to discuss with them. I dim the lights and put on some gentle music. We slip under the covers together. Cuddling with them, I do my best to try and explain, in an age-appropriate manner, truths that I don't even understand.

I begin by admitting that you were sad for quite a long time before you died. They never really knew this because I did such a good job at hiding it from them. I suggest that you had an illness called depression. Depression, I explain, is when you feel so sad that nothing seems to have color or use or meaning anymore. Sometimes this happens because a little part of the brain stops working properly; the part that helps people to feel happy. This is similar to other diseases, for example, people whose eyes or legs might not work properly. They can go to the doctor or take tablets to try and make it better again, but that doesn't always help. I sigh as I point out that you didn't want to go to the doctor or take tablets for your depression. You said you had lived a happy life and didn't feel as if it was going to be happy any longer. So you decided that you didn't want to be alive anymore. It was a very hard decision because you knew how much we would miss you. I tell them that you swam as far as you could go out to sea so that you would be so tired and just fall asleep in the water. Then I say, "Daddy killed himself. He wanted to die."

At this point, the girls are both staring at me in horror. Rose's face creases up. She starts sobbing. Jane has tears brimming in her eyes. I apologize for not telling them sooner because I wanted to protect them. I promise that you loved them so much, more than the sun, the moon, the stars, and the sea, and that it had nothing to do with them. They must know that. You tried your best to make yourself better without a doctor, but you couldn't do it in the end. You were too tired of being unhappy. I tell them that you said you were sorry and that you would always love us and be with us in spirit.

By now, they are both sobbing and the questions begin. Rose asks me why we couldn't help you. I reply that Ruth and I did try to help; we tried everything we could think of doing. Jane asks me what we did. I mention that we tried to get you to see a doctor; we begged you to take medicine. I also asked you to come home. Jane questions me about the time you were in hospital. I confess that you had tried to drown yourself then too, but someone had saved you. The next time you made sure that you swam so far out so that no one could save you. You didn't want to be saved. Jane wonders if you are still in heaven because you killed yourself. My response is that of course you are in heaven; everyone goes to heaven, even sick people. I make sure that they know that killing oneself is not something that people should do. It's okay to feel sad but if the sadness becomes your whole life or goes on for a long time, it is important to talk about it or go to a therapist for help. Jane whimpers that she'd rather not believe it because it's too sad and she'll think about it when she's older. I agree that that is probably a good idea.

Rose howls as she recalls a seemingly unrelated time when you were still at home in Durban. You had asked her if she preferred to go out to the shops with you or stay at home with me. Jane had decided to go along and Rose chose to stay at home. Crying now, she tells me that she has changed her mind. "I wanted to go, see Mom? I wanted to go." she wails. I kiss them and sing them both to sleep.

At times, I am still not sure that I actually accept that you are gone. I can go through a day as usual and still half expect to see a message from you. Even though I don't sense you around that much anymore, I go out onto the veranda most nights and chat to the empty rocking chair. Sometimes I babble on about life. On occasion I light a cigarette and say, "I bet you miss this!" I watch carefully for signs of movement, the cat getting a fright or flickering lights; anything. But there is only the quietness of the garden and my words to you.

51

It is a cold, wintry night in July. The wind comes in gusts, at times shaking the trees so hard that branches fall onto the tin roof with a crash. I am dressing to go out to a fortieth birthday party when the doorbell rings. My neighbor stands at the gate, holding a small box. Inside is our deaf white kitten, Cloud. She has been run over by a speeding car outside our house. Cloud looks peaceful as if she is asleep. I carry the box inside and have to break the news to Jane and Rose. Jane starts sobbing. Cloud was her favorite pet.

The girls take turns holding the tiny lifeless kitten. I let them stroke and kiss her for a while. My neighbor digs a large hole in the garden, next to our Leopard tree. The girls tell Cloud that you will look after her now. Jane doesn't stop crying. We put the kitten back into the box and the girls add flowers and a photograph of themselves. Jane lowers the box into the hole. After a moment's silence, when Jane is ready, she covers the box with sand. Both girls write cards and draw pictures of cats to put on the small grave, along with a few of their favorite toys and some more flowers.

Jane asks me to read her a bedtime story about a cat. Every night she used to hold Cloud when she went to bed. Now she complains mournfully that she can't sleep without her little companion. "Poor Cloud," she wails. I tell her that I suspect that Cloud had probably not even noticed the car and the next moment she woke up in heaven. She would have been so surprised because, for the first time, she would be able to hear. Jane cries herself to sleep. I look at the pictures and letters from you that are stuck up next to the bed. I feel so lost. I ask you to please look after our little friend. As I leave the room, I think I hear the sound of the bell on Cloud's little blue collar.

Death must be one of the cruelest things. People are born into this world, thrown together with other human beings and learn to love them. Then they are taken away. One of the only ways for me to try and grasp this bitter truth is to view it from an eternal perspective. I fling myself into this by reading book after book on death and the afterlife. I have even started visiting psychics, though it goes against my skeptical nature.

We were in Cape Town visiting Ruth and Bradley last month when I saw my first psychic. I crept into the dusty little bookshop on Long Street, not quite knowing what to expect. Sitting across from a jolly-faced woman, I concentrated on keeping a dead-pan face so as not to give away any clues. All I let on was that my husband had recently passed. Her reading was long and surprisingly accurate and authentic. She revealed many details that no stranger could be aware of such as the fact that I homeschool my children.

She had engaged my attention by the time she alleged that you were in counseling on the other side. The transition was not traumatic, she said; you didn't feel anything. It was your time to go. Although you were a strong soul, you weren't finished in this life. It was like going around in a circle for you. You still have many things to learn. She confirmed that your soul loved me very much. By the time you left, you knew that you had given me all you could. Our contract was concluded. Something else she said stood out to me. She told me, "The book that you want to write, you've got to continue."

The next psychic I visited picked up immediately that there

had been a death around me recently, a loved one. I told her that it was my husband. She enquired whether you died of an overdose. When I answered no, she claimed that was odd, as she had the feeling that you fell asleep. She mentioned that, around your birthday, you had become extremely depressed. She claimed she saw you swimming out into the ocean towards the moon. Then I thought about the sleeping tablets. I hadn't told her how you died.

The one message I had from you was when visiting an eccentric old woman. Her room was filled with dolphins and fairies and she could apparently communicate with spirits. Despite my initial reservations, I was surprised by what I heard. She told me there was a gentleman in the room who was difficult to understand. I immediately knew it was you. She announced that you kept babbling something about a son. When I shook my head, she chuckled that you had apologized for confusing her. She paused, cocked her head to the side and then said, "Okay. He says girls, two daughters. He wants them to know that he loves them very much." She added that you also wanted me to know that you do visit and try to help, but it's frustrating because no one can see you. I laugh. Just like something you would say. Then you disappeared. "One more thing," said the eccentric woman, "there is a dog, a dog that's passed over is being well looked after by a relative." Mr. Spooks!

It was later, when I was relaying the story to a friend, that it became clearer. I looked at her in surprise as she burst into tears before gasping, "SUN! Not son. The sun, the moon, the stars, and the sea."

Of course. How could I not have picked that up? I told the girls about the woman who can talk to spirits and gave them your message.

If I raise myself up high above the earth, up to a place where everyone remembers the eternal, where it is understood that time here on earth is only for a brief moment, if I sit perched like a bird on a wire from that high up, I sometimes understand death. It looks the tiniest bit less harsh from up there. I think about the circle of life; how everything has a time.

But from down here, on the veranda, I don't have that view. Death is cruel. It hurts and steals and grabs. It separates and it's forever. I will never see you again in this life as my husband or the father of Jane and Rose. Bugger whatever is after that. Here and now, I have lost you.

52

I drop Rose at dance class, do the dreaded errands, fetch Rose, go home, make dinner, feed the animals, and eventually sit down with a glass of red wine, a cigarette, and a thick brown envelope. The girls are watching a movie. I have been carrying the envelope around for a few hours today without opening it yet. It's your post-mortem report that I collected from the lawyer's offices this afternoon. It has taken seven months to arrive. Sitting outside in the warm evening air, I nervously slide out the papers. Inhaling deeply, I begin reading the alien text.

Corpse. Adult white male. Estimated to be 33 years old. Certified dead. Body. Heavy edematous lungs. Rib Fractures. *Perinephric haematoma.* Cause of death consistent with drowning.

I get a reflex shiver when I read the words, "a monochromatic professional tattoo which reads 'Rosie Jane' over the medial aspect of the left forearm" and "the back of the body is covered in sand and small fragments of broken seashells." On that day in the morgue when Ruth and I came to identify your body, I knew it was you. But reading about your Rosie Jane tattoo makes this unexpectedly cold and real. When I read that your heart was heavier than average, I disintegrate into tears.

Calming myself, I try to make sense of the medical terms. I read it through again, this time with a dictionary. I want to understand every word. This takes me quite a while and makes no difference. One fact remains. Your body died. It lay in the Salt River state morgue. Someone had to cut it open and examine it as if you were a piece of meat at the butchery. Next to most of your body parts listed is the word, 'unremarkable.'

Nose: unremarkable. Ears: unremarkable. Mouth: unremarkable. Tongue: unremarkable. Muscles: unremarkable. Sternum: unremarkable.

No! Stop. I almost scream out aloud and quickly feel for another cigarette. There was nothing unremarkable about you.

You were an average middle-class kid and would have lived an average middle class life except that you didn't do average, middle, or class. Sensual, intelligent, unpredictable and easily bored you used to think that you were larger than death, taunting the power of mortality as proof of life. You carried many friends across the stages of your life. Each was mesmerized by your fervor but never willing to get as close to the flame as you did. There was a calculation to your extremes but whether it was a sober you who pulled the strings in the end or whether you lost yourself in the shadows, I do not know. Perhaps it was a bit of both.

Yesterday, when the dictaphone that Jane took from your house broke, she cracked. She loved listening to your voice, the snippets of story ideas and rough renditions of songs you were composing. She would, on occasion, place it under her pillow so that you could sing her to sleep. I put it back into her memory box and let her have a good cry. Both girls have memory boxes filled with letters, photographs, the stones you gave them from the end of the world, and other cherished reminders. Rose's contains the glass marble that you found in the barn of your derelict childhood home. Whenever they feel upset we look through the boxes and I allow them to cry for as long as they need to. Jane continued to sob about how she wished you would be able to come to her end of year ballet concert and then on to how she misses her best friend.

Amanda still lives in the corner house with Barry and her two children. I bump into her occasionally at the grocery store or at a gig and I can't help but notice the sadness swimming in her huge green eyes. They are vacant too, as if somehow, they will never be occupied again. Her smile is slow and sorry and a mixture of regret and unrequitedness trickles off of her cinnamon skin. I don't wish her any harm. How can I detest her for loving you?

Tonight when I get out my green backpack to pack for a short spring break in the mountains, I discover four smooth acorns in the front pocket. It hits me that the last time I used the backpack was in Cape Town with you. All the oak trees, lanes, and walks, come flooding in as I stroke them. I'm not sure if you or I found these but to me they represent the four of us; our family. Four perfect acorns. With all our flaws, differences, and insecurities, we were still perfect. Nothing is less than perfect. There are no mistakes. I put the acorns next to the bed, as a reminder of you. Not that I could ever forget.

53

"This year the dad died, the cat died, the housekeeper died…This RAT CAN'T DIE!" I emphasize as I place Magic on the silver table. The vet looks at me wide-eyed and promises to do his best to save Magic our rat. But three tumors and five days later, Magic breathes her last breath in the tattered pink handbag home that Jane and Rose gave her. Hers is the fourth death in ten months.

There are food items in my fridge that are old. Some are rotten. I see them every time I open it, but I don't care. There's too much to do. Unopened mail lies on my desk. There is dust and dog hair everywhere. To-do lists get longer. They creep around behind me like dark shadowy reminders all day and follow me to bed at night. I sleep in my clothes; it's one less thing to do when I wake up. You died. The housekeeper died. I have to do everything myself. Business is quiet and there is not enough money. It's the end of the month again, and I don't think I am managing.

I start playing Sudoku, Tetris, and Word Scramble for nights on end. Anything where I can arrange the words, numbers, or shapes and make them fit. Sort them out. Make them ordered. Make them make sense. I can't go to sleep until I have won over and over again. I cannot sleep on a loss. Things must be just right. I sleep with patterns and numbers in my head easier than I sleep with my thoughts and memories that haunt me. I tidy the house, all day, every day. It must be perfect; everything in its place. I start shouting at the girls when they leave one thing out of order. I can't cope with chaos. My other self – the one that watches me – can see what I'm doing, how ridiculous it is. But I can't seem to help this self. I wonder if I have become obsessive. Compulsive. No, I'm far too sensible for that. I stop inviting children over to play, they will make too much mess. I lock all the toys away and bring out only a few at a time.

Some nights I ask if you ever thought about how it would really be for me, without you. I listen for your voice in the rustle of the garden leaves, in the hot summer wind. I can't hear anything. I listen for your voice in my heart. Mostly I reason that I'm imagining it. Imagining what you might say if you could. I am afraid of being alone with all these responsibilities. At times my fear turns into anger that is directed towards those closest to me – the girls. They don't deserve it. Of course I realize that. But I keep on doing it. So many times you asked me to love the girls. I sit outside on the veranda and apologize to you. Sorry I shouted. Sorry I can't manage. Then I come inside and kiss their sleeping foreheads and tell them I'm sorry. I will try harder.

Late one night, after my thousandth Sudoku, I finally admit that I am not coping. I'm taking it out on the innocent girls; the girls who have lost a dad. They only have me. I need help. As synchronicity would have it, Jane gets a severe ear infection and I rush her to the doctor. He asks me how I am doing. I admit, not well. The doc suggests that two years of stress may well have depleted my serotonin levels. He asks if I would consider antidepressants. Without a hesitation, I answer, "Yes, yes please." Within a few days, I can feel the difference. No more shouting. No more obsessive behavior. I almost hear the wooden house sigh with relief. I sigh with relief. I think the girls do too.

Susie says that stress stops your body from working naturally and that over the past two years I must have completely drained every bit of serotonin for these tablets at such a low dosage to have had such an immediate effect. So it's been a good decision for me, even though it's a surprising one. Who would have guessed the irony that I would be the one so willing to take the tablets when you were the one who needed them so desperately yet refused to even consider taking them?

Things go back to being somewhat normal. My appetite returns. The girls and I spend time reading and learning together. I manage to get all my work done as well as tidy the house. After bedtime stories and cuddles, I'm back to writing furiously again at night. I still have moments of tears but I am able to dry my eyes and press forth.

The girls and I begin a ritual of dancing. We turn up the music and dance our butts off in the lounge, swinging each other around and giggling as we try all sorts of crazy new moves. I dance my way through the silence, through the pain. Music makes the house seem less lonely and I can forget myself for a while.

I take up collage art therapy with Gita. We work from the bottom up, through each of the times in my life, working with colors and ages. Through these sessions, I begin to see myself more clearly. Gradually, I notice how hard I am on myself. How important it is for me to save others, forgetting so easily about myself. I realize for the first time that it is me who needs the saving.

54

Last night I had another dream about you. We were together in a pub. When I turned away for a minute, you were gone. I ran through the shopping center and headed down towards the ocean. I knew that was where you were going. I ran and ran until I found you on the beach. The rest is blurry. But I remember that you had given away all your belongings and were planning to do it again. You were sad and beyond reason.

Every night, I write my story for myself and the girls. I dig and plow through the details and churn up all the dust, trying to make sense of it all. I cough fiercely as I write; but I have to keep going. I have been writing about my struggle to save you. Every time I write about this time, I get sick; as sick as I was when it was happening. Some nights my body responds in different ways and shakes so violently that I can't type. Cellular memory, I guess it is. When I get stuck, I go outside and sit on the veranda and smoke. Most nights I still sit outside and talk to you. The moon peeps through the trees, a silver mist behind thin clouds. I say hello and smile, talking to the moon as if it might be you. It may be silly but it gives you a form; something concrete instead of me talking to thin air.

I visit Susie for a healing. Susie says that my cough is a bark at the world. I'm tired of barking. I'm tired of being sick. To my surprise, while lying on the therapy bed, I find myself travelling hundreds of years back. I don't understand these things; all I know is what I see. I have a lucid vision of a young boy around eight years old. The boy is me. I'm in a dusty village, hiding behind a hut. In front of me stands a large, muscular horse; his legs as high as I am. There is chaos in the village, shouting and people running. I'm desperately trying to grab on to one of the horse's legs in an effort to give my parents a chance to escape from the horseman. But I am unable to do it. I have the sense that they were both killed by the horseman and I was left alone, a street urchin. Susie says that ever since that time, I've been trying to save everyone, everyone except myself.

To try and learn more about myself, my relationship with you and my connection to suicide, I embark on further past life regressions and healing therapies. One woman I visit urges me to continue scribing my book. She informs me that I was a scribe in three other lifetimes and this book will bring healing. During another session I discover that I have taken my own life in many lifetimes. I did this by curling up and refusing to eat or drink until the end came. This was always after the person I loved the most had died and I was left alone. In this lifetime, I am told, one of my purposes is to simply live to a ripe old age.

As I write, a butterfly flutters into my office and settles on the wall. It is easy to lose sight of the good that I know exists. I trudge through busy days without remembering to look for joy in unexpected places. It's an ongoing process, which, I have found, has required some effort. It's taken me almost a year to be able to start cooking again. This is not to say that I didn't feed the girls, but dinners were usually the easiest pasta dishes or scrambled eggs, or sandwiches. I know something's changed because tonight I threw some crab into a pot and made a slow cooked stock with red wine, basil, tomato, leeks, and garlic. I strained it and gently stirred in the cream. Crab Bisque a la Robyn. While I was cooking, I drank a glass of the red wine and listened to music. It felt good.

The girls and I are excited about an overseas holiday we have coming up at the end of February. I was surfing the Internet when I came across an eight-day 'gratitude cruise' around the Caribbean featuring some of my favorite inspirational speakers. One of the speakers is from the movie, *The Secret*.

Five months before this story began, before the words that would change the course of my life; I watched this movie for the first time. It had a profound effect on me and over the past year, the girls and I have watched it together over twenty times. In particular, I loved the idea of carrying a gratitude rock as a continual reminder to be grateful. Acorns have become my gratitude rocks and I carry them around in my pockets. Each time I feel their smoothness, I am reminded of being grateful for everything you gave me.

When I saw the dates of the cruise, I knew in my heart that we had to go. It will be held over the first anniversary of your death. What better way to spend that time, I thought, than out on the expansive ocean, celebrating life and gratitude.

I am using half of your life insurance money for the trip. Your family is frustrated by this, concerned about me spending so much money on a holiday when we don't have enough to pay the bills. But I can't let that money disappear on bread and milk. I want to use it on something that is meaningful; something the girls and I will remember for the rest of our lives. Our cruise will be followed by ten days in Orlando at Disney World. The girls deserve this after all they've been through. I look forward to being a child again too; three excited kids on a great adventure.

As another reminder to be thankful, I have just had my second tattoo done. I chose the Chinese characters for 'thank you' and had them tattooed on my wrist. I did this so that every time I use my hand I will remember to be grateful for everything in my life.

55

It rains in February. Some nights, like tonight, it pours. I love the sound of the rain on the tin roof. The musty smell of this old house and the cigarette I'm smoking all remind me of you. Sometimes I feel lonely, but not for lack of people around me. Just for lack of you.

The rain falls harder now, pounding onto the corrugated roof and drenching the garden I've only remembered to water twice in the last year. A year has gone by so quickly, yet every day has lingered. The night-times are long, too, but I don't mind them that way being a night owl by nature. Our girls are extraordinary little creatures. They are part of you. The part I'll always have. Rose turns six next month and I want to wrap myself around her as you used to do. You were good at that; wrapping yourself around the things you loved, becoming almost one with them. It's been one year since I've seen you and I need to start living. It's time for me to start breathing freely; to make up for all the time I didn't, and for the time you haven't.

I follow the rhythm of the rain out onto the veranda so that I can be closer to it, smell it. I sit here most nights, smoking cigarettes and talking to you. The rain calls me nearer. I want to be in it; to have it wash over me. The first heavy drops that hit me are a shock. Cold. Wet. Then the surprise turns to pleasure as it begins to skip over my skin. I laugh as I lift up my hands in the air and turn in slow circles to the beat of the rain. Symbolically turning the hands of time, I rewind.

We sit happily on the veranda. The girls are young. They giggle in their splash pool while you play jazz on the guitar. We are laughing. There are dogs and cats, a beautiful garden; and it is all perfect. There is love, so much love. And there is hope.

Laughter turns to sobs that cannot be heard above the pelting. My clothes are drenched and so I peel them off. I can dance naked in the rain. I am doing it, my naked white body glowing under the green garden lights. As I turn up my face to taste the rain, the tears wash away. It is pure pleasure. The girls discover me and scurry out ripping off their clothes as they do. Finally, giggling and freezing, we scamper into the house to run a hot bath.

I only just finished the green and white mosaic of waves around the bathtub. A project I started at the same time that this story began. As I placed the finishing pieces of glass, I completed my story, a collage of the past two years. I added the washed and worn beach glass I collected with you in Cape Town soon after you came out of the hospital. I remember that day on the beach; sitting and searching for my treasures in the sun while you splashed in the shallows with the girls. I didn't know it then, but those were to be their last memories of you.

That day, as the four of us sat next to the sea, I couldn't have foreseen that the same sea would carry you away from me, my dear friend. That it would be the portal to your peace. I miss you unbearably, Stuart. I will miss you always. Someday I will meet with you again. For you, this will be like the blink of an eye. For me, it will be a lifetime.

Once the girls are asleep, I sit down on the veranda. Carefully, I open the square white envelope and slide out the contents – an art postcard, a couple of photographs and a compilation CD.

This is the parcel you sent to Leila the day before you died and I received from my friend in England three months later. You never guessed that I was Leila. I reread the message inside the CD insert.

23 February 2007

Dear Leila

Sorry I had to go and expire on you; maybe we could've had a whisky one day in the future (which I can see). Here are some songs. Love is bigger than life and I sincerely hope you will love in this life. From your few fragile words, I expect you will.

Stuart

PS I think you should write a book - you know how to.

Afterword

It took me four years to write and edit this book. During that time, I worked several jobs from home while homeschooling Jane and Rose. I wrote at night when they were asleep. There were many times that I wanted to give up but something kept spurring me on.

In mid 2011, I finally finished my memoir and made the decision to self-publish. The manuscript was sent to an editing company for a final check. I was disappointed that the comments I received back were mostly about Stuart's depression, rather than on grammar or writing style. This caused me to launch into another investigation into depression and suicide. It was during this research that I stumbled across a term that I had not previously looked at. I followed the link. As I read page after page until the early hours of the morning, my jaw literally hung open. It was as if I was reading about Stuart. Four years after he died, and in not seeking a label, I found one that described him more accurately than anything else I had come across – Borderline Personality Disorder.

It's too late, of course, for any kind of diagnosis. I am merely speculating about the possibility of a condition that may or may not have been partly present. I was somewhat calmed to read that medication does not cure this disorder; it is used only to treat certain symptoms, such as depression, with the idea of helping a patient benefit from the long-term therapy that is required. Sadly, this disorder has a 10% successful suicide rate.

I know I might seem naïve, to think that Stuart was unique, just his own person, but in a way, I still believe this. Label or no label. There were times that I didn't know what to believe, but I always believed in him. I believed him to be his best, even when he showed me his worst. I saw through all of the surface facades into the heart of a man that was good. As readers, you will have all sorts of different feelings that my story evokes in you from your individual experiences. Many people may have their own ideas about how I should have handled the bizarre situations I found myself in. Some may find my story unbelievable. If you were looking for a book with a happy ending, this is not it, but sometimes in life, the happy ending unfolds, not through circumstances, but from what we learn from those circumstances.

Writing my story has been a huge part of my own healing process which will continue for the rest of my life. I have persevered with my quest for inner peace and will accept nothing less than a life that is rich and meaningful. Jane and Rose and I are happy and healthy and we have a multitude of dreams for a wonderful future ahead.

Thank you for sharing my journey.

Resources

The following may be useful for further reading and help.

Books:
On Grief and Grieving by Elizabeth Kübler-Ross and David Kessler – Scribner 2007
Life on the Other Side by Sylvia Browne and Lindsay Harrison – Signet 2001

Websites:
Grief.com – Because Love Never Dies…
http://grief.com
Suicide Prevention, Awareness, and Support
http://www.suicide.org
Befrienders Worldwide
http://www.befrienders.org
Samaritans
http://www.samaritans.org

Helplines:
24-hour, toll-free suicide prevention lines in the United States
1-800-SUICIDE (1-800-784-2433)
1-800-273-TALK (1-800-273-8255)
24-hour, toll-free help line in South Africa
Lifeline 0861-322-322

Acknowledgements

I would like to acknowledge all the wonderful people who have offered me immense support and been the wind beneath my wings during the past four years of writing. Thanks to Gretha, Neil, Leigh, Darren, and Jess who offered invaluable feedback on early drafts. A most special thanks to my incredible editor, Roxanne Hughes, who worked tirelessly with me through the final edit and without whom I don't think I would have ever finished. Thank you, Lee, Dad, Lynn, Mary, and Deborah for combing the completed manuscript for any errors.

I would also like to express my thanks to the artists and designers who volunteered assistance with the book cover. Thanks to Roger Jardine for your incredible graphic design talent, and to Dave Southwood for the use of the cover photograph, which is an actual photo of the beach where Stuart drowned. And thank you Kobus for the kind use of your story, 'Farewell at Vetch's Pier.'

I am deeply grateful to all of my dear friends, near and far, for your encouragement through the writing and publishing process, for believing in me, and for never allowing me to give up.

To Mom and Dad – you continue to teach me the value of what truly matters in life. Thank you for your unwavering faith and support.

To Stuart – for everything including the powerful gift of grief.

And lastly, to my two lovely girls, Jane and Rose, without whom I may not have had the will to carry on. Thank you for sharing me with my computer for the four years it took me to write. Most of all, thank you for being the delightful joy of my days and for sharing this lifetime with me.

Made in the USA
Coppell, TX
09 October 2020